Lord, I Believe

Lord, I Believe

60 devotions for your troubled heart

Lori Hatcher

Our Daily Bread Publishing

Interior design by Michael J. Williams

ISBN: 978-1-64070-425-1

Library of Congress Cataloging-in-Publication Data Available

Printed in the United States of America
25 26 27 28 29 30 31 32 / 8 7 6 5 4 3 2 1

To our faithful God, who calls us to believe
and meets us in our unbelief.
"Without faith it is impossible to please God,
because anyone who comes to him must
believe that he exists and that he rewards
those who earnestly seek him."
Hebrews 11:6

Contents

I believe . . .

God will help me overcome my unbelief—*Mark 9:24* 11
God delights in me—*Zephaniah 3:17* 14
Jesus seeks the wandering—*Matthew 18:12* 16
I can trust the Good Shepherd—*Psalm 23:1* 19
Strength comes when I embrace my weakness —*2 Corinthians 12:10* 22
I can have heavenly joy—*1 Peter 1:8* 25
Jesus intercedes for me—*1 John 2:1* 28
God sees my secret tears—*Psalm 56:8* 31
I don't have to earn God's love—*Romans 5:8* 33
The Holy Spirit will convict and transform me —*John 16:8* 35
I can hope in God—*Psalm 42:11* 38
God created the world with us in mind —*1 Timothy 6:17* 41
God can comfort others through me —*2 Corinthians 1:3–4* 43
God calls believers to unity in Christ—*John 17:22–23* 45
God's mercy never ends—*Lamentations 3:22* 48
I can have peace—*Isaiah 26:3* 50

I believe . . .

God created me as I am for a purpose —*Ephesians 2:10* 52

My labor isn't in vain—*1 Corinthians 15:58* 54

I'm never alone—*Psalm 139:7* 56

I can be bold—*Acts 4:29* 59

Jesus is my friend—*Matthew 11:19* 62

Our suffering will end—*Romans 8:18* 64

Every day is Good Morning—*Psalm 118:24* 67

God is always at work—*John 5:17* 70

I can glorify God in my death—*John 21:19* 72

God answers prayer—*James 5:16* 75

God will guide me through life—*Psalm 25:4–5* 77

The Holy Spirit abides with me forever —*John 14:16–17* 79

I can be great in God's kingdom—*Matthew 20:26* 81

I have a choice—*Habakkuk 3:18* 84

Jesus is coming back—*John 14:3* 87

Jesus is God—*Hebrews 1:8* 90

God can restore—*Joel 2:25* 92

God is trustworthy—*Deuteronomy 33:27* 95

I should pray—*1 Thessalonians 5:17* 97

I've received Christ's righteousness —*2 Corinthians 5:21* 99

God calls me to practice hospitality—*1 Peter 4:9* 101

God calls me to praise Him—*Psalm 150:6* 104

God can transform my ending —*Philippians 3:13–14* 107

God wants me to be part of a church —*Hebrews 10:25* 110

I'll find God—*Jeremiah 29:13* 113

I believe . . .

God never wastes suffering—*2 Corinthians 4:17* 115

I exist to glorify God—*Romans 6:10* 117

God is with me even in death—*Psalm 23:4* 119

God calls me to share what He's done for me —*Psalm 66:16* 121

God calls me to love Him unconditionally —*Matthew 22:37* 124

Jesus welcomes His children into His arms —*Matthew 19:15* 126

If I resist the Devil, he will flee—*James 4:7* 128

God protects me through the local church —*Galatians 6:1* 131

I must recognize I'm lost to be saved—*Luke 5:32* 134

God calls me to study His Word—*2 Timothy 2:15* 137

God calls me to not complain—*Philippians 2:14–15* 140

God takes no pleasure in the death of the wicked —*Ezekiel 33:11* 143

God loves me—*Ephesians 3:17–18* 146

God's people must be kind and gentle —*2 Timothy 2:24* 148

My heart will deceive me—*Proverbs 3:5–6* 151

The gospel has the power to save—*Romans 1:16* 154

Jesus prayed for me—*John 17:20* 157

God will draw near to me—*James 4:8* 159

God promises I'll spend eternity with Him —*Revelation 22:6* 161

How to Have a Relationship with Christ 165

Notes 167

About the Author 169

I believe . . .

God will help me overcome my unbelief

Immediately the boy's father exclaimed, "I do believe; help me overcome my unbelief!"
Mark 9:24

When was the last time you struggled to believe?

Today? Yesterday? Every day?

If we're honest, most of us will answer, "Often."

When we struggle with our jobs, our health, or our marriages, we wonder if God will see us through. When our loved one languishes in a hospital bed or our prodigal child roams the streets doing God knows what, the icy grip of faithlessness squeezes our hearts and takes our breath away.

When we come to God again and again with the same request and nothing changes, our faith wobbles: Maybe I'm wasting my time. Maybe God doesn't care. Or worse—maybe this situation is so bad, so sad, or so broken even God can't fix it.

Such was the case with the man in Mark 9. This man was living a parent's nightmare. A demon had controlled his son since he was a tiny boy. It would twist his little body with convulsions, paralyze his muscles, and throw him to the ground as he foamed at the mouth. Sometimes the father would hear noises and come running, only to discover the demon had flung his son into the fire or into the water.

One day, the man heard stories about a teacher who had fed a multitude and healed a blind man. Maybe, just maybe, He could help his son. So he set out for the teacher's camp.

But Jesus wasn't there.

His disciples listened to his desperate plea and tried to help. But the evil spirit hung on. Maybe even laughed a little.

By the time the Teacher arrived, a crowd had formed. Scribes and disciples argued. Bystanders offered opinions. The boy sat silently in their midst.

"What are you discussing?" Jesus asked.

"Teacher," the man cried, "I brought you my son, who is possessed by a spirit that has robbed him of speech. Whenever it seizes him, it throws him to the ground. He foams at the mouth, gnashes his teeth, and becomes rigid. I asked your disciples to drive out the spirit, but they could not" (vv. 17–18).

As if on cue, the demon convulsed the boy and flung him to the ground. *Take that, Jesus. This one's mine.*

"If you can do anything," his father begged, "take pity on us and help us" (v. 22).

"'*If* you can'?" said Jesus.

In three words, Jesus asked the heart-piercing question that exposed the father's faith struggle—and ours.

Do we believe Jesus can?

Can He heal? Can He provide? Can He restore? Can He defend?

Sometimes I get so snarled up in the sovereignty of God—Is it His will or isn't it His will—that I forget that faith is believing He *can*. "Without faith it is impossible to please God," Hebrews 11:6 tells us. The faith that pleases God doesn't always know *how* God will act. But it knows God *will* act. And that He'll do what is best.

I don't have to know God's will for every situation to pray in faith. Faith isn't knowing the outcome. Faith is knowing God.

"Everything is possible for one who believes," Jesus reminded the father (v. 23).

With the honesty that comes from staring into the all-knowing face of God, the man exclaimed, "I do believe; help me overcome my unbelief!" (v. 24).

We can say the same: Father, I trust You to work all things together for good for those who love You and are called according to Your purposes (Romans 8:28).

On that day long ago, Jesus responded to a father's wobbly faith by doing a miracle. He's still doing miracles today.

I hope *Lord, I Believe: 60 Devotions for Your Troubled Heart* will help you stake your faith on the firm foundation of God's Word—and believe.

I believe . . .

God delights in me

He will take great delight in you; in his love he will no longer rebuke you, but will rejoice over you with singing.

Zephaniah 3:17

When you picture God looking at you, what expression do you imagine?

For much of my Christian life, I pictured God's loving eyes displaying a hint of disappointment. "Good try, honey," I could almost hear Him say. I imagined a benevolent smile tag-teaming with a quiet sigh. *Bless her heart. Someday she'll get it right.*

Most days, the smile never reached His eyes. You nailed it today, but you'll mess up tomorrow. I know you will. And I did.

On really bad days, when I knew my sin had hurt Him, those all-seeing eyes shimmered with tears.

I knew Jesus died to pay for my sins, but I also knew He expected something of me now that I was a Christian. In my mind, this *something* was perfect behavior. Whenever I fell short of that impossible standard, I felt God's disappointment. My spirit shriveled under His imagined disapproval.

Then I had grandchildren. Four perfect grandchildren.

Every time I think of them, I smile. Sometimes my husband catches me grinning and asks, "What are you smiling about?"

"The grandbabies," I say, and he understands.

Funny thing about grandchildren. They're perfect, even when they're not.

One of ours is prone to theatrics. When she loses a game, she raises her voice in protest and collapses in a heap. Another dumps the entire bin of Beanie Babies in the middle of my floor—every time—and argues about cleaning them up. Still another can spill a drink almost before I finish pouring it. The last wants whatever toy the other sibling is playing with, even if he set that same toy aside just two minutes ago.

Not much surprises me about my grandchildren. I know they're immature, sometimes selfish, and messy—very messy. But they're my grandchildren. And I delight in them.

I'm learning God feels this way about us. He knows we're immature, often selfish, and very messy. But we're His children. He delights in us.

We're the apple of His eye (Psalm 17:8). More valuable than the birds (Matthew 10:31). So loved that He sacrificed His only Son for us (Romans 5:8).

"The LORD your God is with you, the Mighty Warrior who saves. He will take *great delight* in you . . . [and] will rejoice over you with singing" (Zephaniah 3:17, emphasis added).

Do I want my grandchildren to grow in maturity and behavior? Of course. But this doesn't change my affection for them.

Does God want me to grow in maturity and behavior? You bet. But my imperfections don't keep Him from delighting in me.

Stop a minute and think of the person you love most.

Now look at your smile in the mirror.

This is what God looks like when He thinks of you.

Embrace the Truth: God delights in us.

Declare Your Faith: Lord, I believe the joy You feel in me has nothing to do with my performance. You delight in me because I'm Your child. And You not only love me, You like me. Help me receive this and live in light of it. Help me silence the voices of condemnation and insecurity I often feel and rest instead in the security of Your exuberant, joy-filled love. Amen.

I believe . . .

Jesus seeks the wandering

What do you think? If a man owns a hundred sheep, and one of them wanders away, will he not leave the ninety-nine on the hills and go to look for the one that wandered off?

Matthew 18:12

Muffy was a runner.

The lady at the shelter had warned Matt when he picked her out of a host of dogs needing homes.

"Her previous owner turned her in because he tired of chasing her all over town," she said. "She also has a fondness for chewing things. She's afraid of thunder, and, well, we're working on housebreaking her."

Matt looked at Muffy. Muffy looked at Matt. One of her ears stood up while the other flopped. Her wiry coat was an odd mixture of grey, brown, and black, and the tip of her tail bent at an awkward angle. As he watched, she gnawed a bar of her crate.

"I'll take her."

The first few weeks were rough, even for a dog lover like Matt. Muffy chewed his favorite pair of Docksiders, the leg of his entertainment center, and the corner of every box in the house. One night, he found her sitting on the dining room table devouring the pizza he'd brought home for dinner. But she followed him everywhere and slept beside him, snoring gently into his ear.

One day the bug man failed to latch the gate, and Muffy was gone. Like a BB out of a pellet gun, she rocketed out of the yard, headed for who knows where. Matt chased her through the neighborhood for an hour. It was the first of many escapes.

Sometimes she came home in an hour or two, head hung low and crooked tail drooping. Other times, Matt went looking for her. Occasionally, she'd run so far she couldn't find her way back home.

One time, the longest time, Muffy disappeared for three weeks. Matt finally found her five miles away, dirty, hungry, and eating out of a trash can. When he called her, she came toward him, limping from a sand spur caught between her toe pads. He scooped her up, soiling his white button-down. Muffy covered his face with slobbery doggy kisses, then rested her tired head on his shoulder with a grateful sigh.

Matt's commitment to Muffy, in a small way, mirrors Jesus's commitment to us.

We weren't looking for Jesus when He chose us to be His own. He took the initiative. He didn't need us, but we sure needed Him. Adopting us into His forever family, He promised to meet our every need. He loves us—lavishly, sacrificially, joyfully.

But sometimes we're like Muffy. We love to run. Something shiny catches our eye, and we dash after it with nary a backward glance. Home is nice, but excitement beckons. Other times, we simply wander. Without intending to, we allow busyness, laziness, or apathy to lure us from His side.

Always the Good Shepherd, God leaves the fold and sets off into the darkness of our sin to woo us back. He lavishes us with the grace of forgiveness and draws us into His embrace. He lifts us onto His shoulders and carries us home, rejoicing.

I long to live every day close to God. I think you do too. But if we become deceived by sin, self, or Satan, God won't abandon us. He'll come looking for us, and when He finds us, He'll welcome us back home.

Embrace the Truth: God won't abandon us when we wander away. He'll come looking for us.

Declare Your Faith: Lord, I believe if I run or wander away, You'll come looking for me. You're committed to me on the days I delight You and on the days I fail You. I want to live close by Your side, but I know there will be times when I'll get distracted or deceived. Thank You for not abandoning me in my sinfulness. Give me a tender heart that recognizes and confesses my sin quickly so You can restore me. I love You so much. I want to please You in everything I do. Amen.

I believe . . .

I can trust the Good Shepherd

The LORD is my shepherd; I shall not want.
Psalm 23:1 ESV

My friend, April, is a shepherdess.[1] Really. She and her husband own a farm on the banks of the Cape Fear River in North Carolina. They have goats, chickens, cows, and sheep. And several dogs to keep them all in line.

April didn't set out to be a shepherdess. She has a degree in human medicine, and her lifetime calling is to care for people as a physician. But somehow, there they are, the proud owners of a farm.

I suspect the same qualities that make April a really good PA also make her a really good shepherdess. April loves her sheep and cares for them well.

One winter day, while making the rounds of their property, April discovered a surprising patch of green grass tucked along the edge of the pasture. This sunny spot had somehow escaped the killing frost that had affected the rest of the property.

She knew her sheep would love to have some fresh grass to eat after months of dried hay. She jumped on her all-terrain vehicle, rode to where the sheep were grazing, and led them to the pasture. Like kids at an all-you-can-eat pizza buffet, her sheep filled their mouths with the tasty treat as April grinned. Their joy made her joy complete.

April's sheep are much better sheep than I am. Even though I know God is my Good Shepherd, I don't always follow Him willingly. If I'd been one of April's sheep, I suspect I'd have asked a thousand questions, requested a soil sample to prove the nutrient content of the grass, and GPSed a road map detailing the exact route she planned to take.

You know the difference between April's sheep and me? They trust their shepherdess.

Ouch.

It hurts to say it, type it, think it, but it's true. Sometimes I don't trust God. When I'm afraid to follow His clear direction or wonder if He's going to take care of me, I show my distrust.

King David, a shepherd himself, penned perhaps the most famous verses on sheep and shepherds when he wrote, "The Lord is my shepherd; I shall not want" (Psalm 23:1 ESV).

This sentence, only nine words, should be all we need to banish our fears and calm our anxious hearts. God is our shepherd. We have nothing to worry about. The End.

But for the skeptical (and faith-trembly) among us, He doesn't stop there. He shows us why we can trust our shepherd.

Our Good Shepherd will

> Feed us (v. 2)
> Give us rest (v. 2)
> Restore our souls (v. 3)
> Guide us in wise paths (v. 3)
> Protect us from evil (v. 4)
> Sustain us (v. 5)
> Minister to us (v. 5)
> Take us home to live with Him forever (v. 6)

When I act like a suspicious sheep, my faithlessness doesn't change a thing about God. He's going to take care of me, whether or not I trust Him. He can't act contrary to His character. He's the Good Shepherd, and He'll always be the Good Shepherd.

But when I fail to trust Him, I hurt myself. I rob myself of the peace that comes with following Him to green pastures and quiet streams. Then I wonder why I'm so scared. And lonely. And confused. Why I'm anxious and spiritually hungry.

April's a good shepherdess. She cares well for her sheep. God's an even better Good Shepherd. He laid down His life for His sheep (John 10:11).

The only question that remains, then, is, Am I a good sheep?

"The sheep listen to his voice. He calls his own sheep by name and leads them out. When he has brought out all his own, he goes on ahead of them, and his sheep follow him because they know his voice" (vv. 3-4).

I want to be that kind of sheep.

Embrace the Truth: God has given us every reason to trust Him as our Good Shepherd.

Declare Your Faith: Lord, I believe You are the Good Shepherd and worthy of my trust. I praise You for how You've always taken care of me. When I let You, You guide me, protect me, and restore me. Thank You. When I'm tempted to fear, remind me of Your faithfulness and love. Help me resist the urge to forge off on my own. Transform me into a good sheep who follows You all the days of my life. Amen.

I believe . . .

Strength comes when I embrace my weakness

When I am weak, then I am strong.
2 Corinthians 12:10

Christianity abounds with upside-down truths.

If you want to live, die (Matthew 10:39). If you want to be first, be last (Mark 9:35). If you want to be the greatest, become a servant (Matthew 20:26).

Consider one of the most upside-down statements of the New Testament, made by the apostle Paul: "When I am weak, then I am strong" (2 Corinthians 12:10).

Paul suffered from an unspecified condition. Most scholars suspect it was a painful eye disease. Others think his challenge was a spiritual opponent who attempted to thwart his ministry. In his second letter to the Corinthians, Paul didn't glamorize his weakness or minimize his pain. He described it as "a messenger of Satan" that tormented him (v. 7).

Perhaps the most vexing aspect of Paul's condition was suspecting he could do much more for God without it.

But could he?

Three times, he begged the Lord to remove his thorn.

Three times God said no.

No? Really God?

Yep.

Why?

"To keep [you] from becoming conceited," God revealed to Paul (v. 7).

God knew that if Paul served Him from a position of strength, he'd fail. Pride would make him depend on his natural abilities instead of God's enabling. He'd follow his human instincts and make decisions based on his intellect instead of relying on God to direct him.

God knew Paul would be most effective in the kingdom if he labored from a position of weakness.

Imagine this.

"My grace is sufficient for you," God told Paul, "for my power is made perfect in weakness" (v. 9).

And it was.

With the grace God provided in his affliction, Paul evangelized most of Asia and parts of Europe. He planted many churches despite fierce opposition, sang praises to God from a jail cell, and wrote much of the New Testament while imprisoned for his faith.

Paul accomplished everything God called him to do by relying on God's strength in his weakness.

What hinders you today?

A health condition? A financial challenge? Maybe you're not the most educated or socially positioned. Perhaps you're "too old." Or "too young." Or your past anchors you to the ground while you long to soar in the Spirit. If you were smarter, younger, richer, or more eloquent, imagine what you could do.

Yet God gives you weaknesses.

"Therefore," Paul concluded, as he accepted with faith the limitations God gave, "I will boast all the more gladly about my weaknesses, so that Christ's power may rest on me" (v. 9).

The same is true for us today. The power of Christ rests on us when we accept our weaknesses and rely on God's strength.

Accepting doesn't mean we don't learn, grow, and overcome. It means we don't allow our weaknesses to keep us from serving God. We don't wait until every obstacle vanishes before we surrender all to Him.

Remember Paul's incredible list of accomplishments? He completed those tasks *in* his weakness, not *in spite of* it.

What might God enable us to do?

Share Christ with our neighbor? Sing praises to God from the prison of a sick bed? Pray for our church's missionaries, Sunday school workers, and pastors? Write faith-filled letters to those who need encouragement?

We probably won't evangelize most of Asia or witness to kings, but we're not Paul. God has other plans for us.

Weaknesses and all.

Embrace the Truth: The power of Christ rests upon us when we surrender our weaknesses to God and rely on His strength.

Declare Your Faith: Lord, I believe that when I am weak, then I am strong. Although it defies reason, I believe You work best through my weakness. Forgive me for being prideful and clinging to my pitiful strength instead of trusting You to empower me. I surrender my weaknesses to You and ask You to fill me with Your mighty strength. Use my limitations to bring You glory. In the strong name of Jesus I ask, amen.

I believe . . .

I can have heavenly joy

You believe in him and are filled with an inexpressible and glorious joy.

1 Peter 1:8

If you'd like to see what controlled chaos looks like, go to your dentist's office the week before Christmas. Teachers and students are on break. College kids return home for the holidays. Government workers use their end-of-the-year vacation days to take time off.

And everyone wants to come to the dentist.

Really.

The two weeks before Christmas are the hardest weeks of the year for dental personnel, which is why we couldn't understand why our coworker, Corinne, was in such a wonderful mood.

When Mr. Hunsaker complained because the X-ray sensor hurt his gums, she apologized and gave him a gentle pat. When three kids scheduled for cleanings all cried when she entered the treatment room, she burst into a silly song and had them all smiling by the end of their appointments. And when Frank, the tobacco-chewing, cigar-smoking redneck, showed up in her chair after a three-year absence, she welcomed him with a smile.

Her cheerfulness defied her circumstances. Finally the receptionist couldn't stand it any longer.

"Why are you in such a good mood?" she asked.

"In three days, my kids will be home," Corinne said. "We're going to join my parents at their mountain cabin and maybe see some snow. The rest of the family will already be there." She squeezed her arms and grinned.

"I haven't seen some of them in years. We always have the best time together." Her smile widened and her eyes danced. "We play games, eat, and tell stories. And then we eat some more. I can't wait."

"This," she said, gesturing to the overflowing waiting room, "is nothing compared to what I have waiting for me."

I pictured Corinne's joyful smile when I read the first chapter of 1 Peter. Peter wrote to Christians dealing with much more than an overfull waiting room and grumpy patients. He reminded believers who'd been driven from their homes and persecuted for their faith, "In [God's] great mercy he has given us new birth into a living hope through the resurrection of Jesus Christ from the dead, and into an inheritance that can never perish, spoil or fade" (1:3–4).

These Christians were experiencing life-threatening peril, yet their gratefulness to God and deep-seated joy remained steadfast. "In all this you greatly rejoice," Peter marveled, "though now for a little while you may have had to suffer grief in all kinds of trials" (1 Peter 1:6).

He assured them of what was to come. "This inheritance is kept in heaven for you, who through faith are shielded by God's power until the coming of the salvation that is ready to be revealed in the last time" (1 Peter 1:4–5). Look forward to experiencing all the glorious aspects of your salvation, Peter said. To the beauty and majesty of heaven. To the living hope we have in God. Let these promises strengthen and keep you.

Most of all, he said, remember who will be there.

"Though you have not seen him, you love him; and even though you do not see him now, you believe in him and are filled with an inexpressible and glorious joy, for you are receiving the end result of your faith, the salvation of your souls" (v. 8–9).

Despite difficult circumstances and severe trials, joy in Jesus welled up in the struggling believers. It can overflow in our hearts as well. This type of joy defies explanation or expression, but we can have it—effervescent and glorious—if we look past this world and into heaven.

Corinne's anticipation of a holiday with her family in a beautiful place made her heart happy and minimized her work trials. How much more joy–filled should we be as we anticipate the glorious eternity that awaits us in heaven with Jesus?

Embrace the Truth: An inexpressible and glorious joy fills our hearts when we look past this world and into heaven at our Savior, Jesus.

Declare Your Faith: Lord, I believe a glorious future awaits me, and this brings me joy. Help this sure and certain hope comfort me when life gets hard. Remind me that soon—perhaps very soon—the things of this earth will grow strangely dim in the light of Your glory and grace.[2] When I grow discouraged, remind me to look toward You and rejoice.

I believe . . .

Jesus intercedes for me

If anybody does sin, we have an advocate with the Father—Jesus Christ, the Righteous One.

1 John 2:1

Jana had never felt so embarrassed. Or so scared.

It all began when she noticed a cell phone lying on the floor in the D building hallway. She recognized it immediately—Mrs. Kavanaugh's. If the deep purple color hadn't triggered her memory, the phone case, bedazzled with rhinestones, sparkles, and a sticker that said, "If you've got it, flaunt it," would have.

She grabbed the phone and headed to her teacher's room, only to find the door closed and the lights off. Jana glanced at her watch. "Ugh. I gotta get to P. E."

Should she leave the phone or take it to the office after class? Mrs. Kavanaugh might need it before then. Surely she'd be right back. Jana decided to leave it—but not on the desk. Someone might steal it.

Holding the glittering phone in one hand, she tugged at the desk drawer with the other and found it unlocked. She reached inside just as light flooded the room. Turning, she found Mr. Robinson, the assistant principal, standing in the doorway.

"What are you doing?" His eyes moved from the open drawer to the phone in her trembling hand. "Never mind," he scowled. "Come with me."

Before they could leave the room, Mr. Carpenter stepped in. He glanced from Jana's frightened face to Mr. Robinson's stormy one.

"What's going on?"

"I caught Jana stealing Mrs. Kavanaugh's phone out of her desk."

"Stealing Mrs. Kavanaugh's phone?" Mr. Carpenter said. "She just picked it up in the hallway." He gestured with his thumb. "I saw her. I stepped in to tell her Mrs. Kavanaugh's in the teacher's lounge."

This story is fictional, but it resembles something that happens every day in heaven. Men, women, and children are falsely accused, not by an assistant principal but by the enemy of their souls.

Revelation 12:10 describes Satan as "the accuser of our brothers and sisters, who accuses them before our God day and night." The first chapters of Job reveal Satan's tactic: to condemn those who belong to God.

The apostle John wrote about why believers can stand firm under his accusations: "My dear children, I write this to you so that you will not sin. But if anybody does sin, we have an advocate with the Father—Jesus Christ, the Righteous One. He is the atoning sacrifice for our sins, and not only for ours but also for the sins of the whole world" (1 John 2:1–2).

Hebrews 7:25 assures us, "He is able to save completely those who come to God through him, because he always lives to intercede for them."

Comparisons break down, and the parallels between Jana's story and ours end with one important difference: Jana was innocent. We aren't. This is why we need an advocate.

As we stand accused before the Judge of our souls, Jesus declares our innocence based on His sinless record, not ours. Satan's accusations have no power over us who have sought God's forgiveness and surrendered our lives to Christ.

Our sins are atoned for. Our guilt is gone.

Embrace the Truth: Satan's accusations have no power over us because Jesus, our advocate, defends us.

Declare Your Faith: Lord, I believe You intercede for me before the Father's throne. When Satan accuses me, You defend me.

Help me remember this whenever I hear his voice reminding me of past sins and trying to defeat me. Enable me to stand strong in the confidence that comes from knowing You are my Savior and my defender.

I believe . . .

God sees my secret tears

You number my wanderings;
Put my tears into Your bottle;
Are they not in Your book?

Psalm 56:8 NKJV

How many secret tears have you shed? The kind no one sees because the sorrow is too deep and too tender?

I cried my first secret tears when I was twelve years old. I was skinny, four inches taller than most of my classmates, and sporting a new short haircut. I was also pretty good at basketball. One day I beat a boy my age at a game of HORSE.

He didn't take it well.

In fact, after he called me a name or two, he questioned my gender. Surely a girl couldn't sink more baskets than a boy. I was already sensitive about being flat-chested and awkward. Being called a boy by a boy hurt more than I cared to admit.

I held my head high on the long walk home, but when I made it to my room and locked the door, the tears flowed. Hot, angry, embarrassed tears. Tears I could never share with anyone. Because who wants to tell that story to your mom, dad, or two younger sisters?

I've cried more than a few secret tears since then. They've poured from deep, aching wounds. The pain of a troubled marriage. The hopelessness of a prodigal child. The ache of an unfulfilled longing known only to God.

These tears wait until the night is dark and the house is quiet. Sometimes they slip silently down my face, trickle into my ears, and soak my pillow. Other times they burst forth in great, wailing sobs.

I take comfort in knowing, despite my efforts to hide them, that Someone sees my secret tears. "You number my wanderings," the psalmist wrote, "Put my tears into Your bottle; are they not in Your book?" (NKJV).

My tenderhearted Father not only sees my tears but He captures them and holds them close. *I see you,* I sense Him whisper. *I feel your hurt and share your pain.* As Jesus was with Mary and Martha at Lazarus's tomb, so He is with me; He shares my sorrow and is moved by my grief.

One day, He promises to wipe every tear from my eyes (Revelation 21:4). Until then, I take comfort in knowing I don't cry in secret. God my Father holds me close. Jesus my Savior weeps with me. God the Holy Spirit comforts me. I am not alone.

Embrace the Truth: God sees our secret tears, captures them, and holds them close.

Declare Your Faith: Lord, I believe You not only see my tears, You treasure them. Because You love me, everything that hurts me hurts You. Thank You for coming close and weeping with me. Your presence reminds me I'm not alone. I can't wait until the day when You wipe every tear from my eyes and I'll never cry again.

I believe . . .

I don't have to earn God's love

God demonstrates his own love for us in this:
While we were still sinners, Christ died for us.

Romans 5:8

Have you ever tried to make someone love you?

When I was in eighth grade, I had a crush on Ricky, the cute baseball player with swooshy hair. I did everything short of reinvent myself to get him to love me.

Baseball never interested me until I sat in front of him in Mr. Weinburg's class. When I discovered he played in the field near my house, I attended every game. When he teased me about my glasses, I ditched them and squinted my way through class. When he made a flattering comment to a classmate about her new haircut, I begged my mom to take me to the salon for a makeover.

All to no avail. Eighth grade ended, and Ricky trotted out of my life.

After I became a Christian, I spent much of my life trying to make God love me. I believed what the Bible said, that I was saved by grace through faith (Ephesians 2:8–9), but I assumed grace only applied to salvation.

It was up to me to meet an impossible standard of perfection. Every year I must serve more and sin less. I could never slow down, reconsider, or step away, because I feared I'd displease the Lord. The way to show my love for Him was to do, do, do. I alternated between periods of frustration and seasons of despair. How much was enough to please Him?

Then I read John 10:10: "The thief comes only to steal and kill and destroy. I came that they may have life and have it abundantly" (ESV). In a moment of spiritual clarity, I realized I wasn't living the abundant life. I was living the oppressed life.

On the heels of this revelation came the glorious truth of Romans 5:8: "God demonstrates his own love for us in this: While we were still sinners, Christ died for us."

For the first time, I understood I didn't have to earn His love or perform to please Him. He proved His love for me on the cross. No annual performance review was going to change that.

He loved me.

Embrace the Truth: I don't have to earn God's love. The nail-scarred hands of Jesus offer it to me as a free gift.

Declare Your Faith: Lord, I believe You love me because of what You endured on the cross. You took the shame, the beating, and the nails for me. You hung there, naked and bleeding, bearing my sin on Your sinless shoulders, and endured the wrath of God so I won't have to. I don't deserve Your love. I can never earn it, but I'm infinitely grateful for it. I love You, Lord.

I believe . . .

The Holy Spirit will convict and transform me

When [the Spirit] comes, he will convict the world concerning sin and righteousness and judgment.

John 16:8 ESV

A strange thing happened after Craig surrendered his life to Christ.

He'd fought it for years. But as he watched his wife, Cathy, transform from a nagging, anxious, often-depressed woman into a sweet person filled with peace and joy, he realized he wanted what she had. Desperately.

Alone in his car on his lunch break one day, he prayed. "God, I've lived my life without You all these years. I'm sorry for the wrong I've done and the people I've hurt. Please come into my life and change me. Amen."

He didn't tell a soul what he'd done, not even Cathy. For a while he wondered if his prayer had accomplished anything. He didn't feel any different. He certainly didn't look any different.

But one day, when he was filling up Cathy's car with gas and charging his company credit card, he heard a voice in his head: What you're doing is wrong. You're stealing from the company.

Craig looked around, but he was alone at the pump. What was that about? He'd been using his company credit card to fill both their tanks for a while now. Everyone padded their expense accounts, and this was his way of compensating for the raise he'd asked for but hadn't gotten last year.

On Sunday, instead of daydreaming about his golf game as he usually did while the pastor preached, Craig found himself strangely interested.

"Paul was writing to Gentile believers in Ephesus who had come to Christ out of deeply sinful lifestyles," Pastor Paul said. "He gave them simple instructions for how to live now that they were God's children: Don't lie. Don't sin in anger. And if anyone has been stealing, he must steal no longer" (Ephesians 4:25–28).

Craig's heart thumped painfully, and sweat broke on his forehead. He shifted to position himself directly behind the lady in front of him, out of the pastor's line of sight. How does he know? I didn't see him at the gas station.

That evening, after the kids were asleep, he confessed it all to Cathy. The parking lot prayer. The voice in his head. The pastor's uncomfortable words. The rock in his stomach.

Cathy cried, hugged him, and cried some more. Then she laughed.

"Why are you laughing?" he said. "I think I'm going crazy."

"You're not going crazy," she said. "That's the Holy Spirit."

At his raised eyebrows, she explained. "When we surrender our life to Christ, the Holy Spirit comes to live inside us. He comforts us, leads us into truth, and convicts us of sin. It's how He transforms us to make us more like Jesus."

He stared at her and shook his head. "This sounds like something from *The Exorcist*. Spirits coming to live inside you. And I certainly don't feel comforted. I feel miserable. I thought surrendering my life to God was supposed to make me feel good."

She laughed and hugged him again. "Did you feel miserable before you prayed that prayer?"

"Only when I got caught."

"See?" Cathy said, blue eyes sparkling. "This is proof your decision was real. You're a new creation in Christ, and God won't let you stay the same. He'll convict you of sin and help you do what's right."

She grabbed her Bible from the table in front of her. "See, it says right here, 'Do you not know that your bodies are temples of the Holy Spirit, who is in you, whom you have received from God? You are not your own'" (1 Corinthians 6:19).

She flipped the pages, slid her finger to a highlighted verse, and read again, "When he comes, he will prove the world to be in the wrong about sin and righteousness and judgment" (John 16:8).

"That bad feeling," she said, "is a really good feeling because it's evidence God is alive in you and working to change you."

"Wow," Craig said. "I never imagined I'd feel so good about feeling bad." He laughed, and Cathy did too. He pointed to her Bible. "Is there anything in there that tells me what to do next?"

"Oh, yes," Cathy answered. "Let me show you 1 John 1:9, one of my favorite verses . . ."

Embrace the Truth: God the Holy Spirit indwells believers, convicts them of sin, and transforms them into Christlike followers.

Declare Your Faith: Lord, I believe Your Holy Spirit indwells me, pointing out sin in my life and helping me change. Wow. It's a mysterious thing, thinking about God living in me. But I'm so grateful I don't have to figure out the Christian life alone or conquer my old ways in my own strength. Thank You for patiently working in me to make me more like Jesus. Make me sensitive to Your nudges and eager to cooperate with what You want to do in and through me. Amen.

I believe . . .

I can hope in God

Why, my soul, are you downcast? Why so disturbed within me? Put your hope in God.

Psalm 42:11

What's the heaviest weight you've ever lifted? My husband, David, used to lift truckloads of tires that weighed fifty pounds each. When he played football in high school, he'd bench-press hundreds of pounds during a workout.

He's pretty strong, but not as strong as weight lifter Hafthor Bjornsson, who set a 2020 world dead lifting record by deadlifting 1,104 pounds.

I've never lifted more than a hundred physical pounds, but I've carried some pretty heavy soul burdens.

Burdens of the soul don't come with barbells or bench presses, nor are they visible, but they are weighty and real. They crush our dreams and our hearts and drive us to the end of ourselves. Casting their shadow over the most joyful days, they linger at the edges of our heart like an unwanted guest at a party. They steal our hope and, if we let them, have the power to shipwreck our faith.

Psalm 42 reflects the heavy soul burden experienced by the psalmist when he penned his verses. Cut off from God's temple and the comfort he received from worshiping with fellow believers, the writer describes how he wrestled with his downcast soul and vacillated between despair and hope.

Ever been there?

Me too.

See how the psalm's author responded when soul-crushing

hopelessness weighed heavy on his heart. Instead of allowing his heartache to turn him away from God, he recognized he needed *more* of God, not less. "My soul thirsts for God, for the living God. When can I go and meet with God?" (v. 2).

I'll confess—sometimes, when my heart feels crushed, I'm tempted to avoid church, saying, "I'm a wreck. I don't want anyone to see me this way." This trick of Satan separates us from our greatest source of support. Worshiping with fellow believers and hearing the truth of God's Word is a powerful cure for soul sickness.

The psalmist also showed how we should talk to ourselves during times of distress. Commentator Matthew Henry describes the man's conversation with himself as "a conflict between sense and faith, sense objecting and faith answering."[3] He didn't deny, suppress, or fail to acknowledge his distress. Rather, he lamented before God and poured out his anguish into God's ever-listening ears.

But he didn't stay in lament. He spoke truth to himself. "Why, my soul, are you downcast? Why so disturbed within me? Put your hope in God" (v. 11). The psalmist reminded himself that the God who was bigger than his trials offered solid, life-sustaining hope if he would receive it.

Hope is what we need most when our hearts despair and our faith trembles. Biblical hope—one that is based on the promises and character of God—will never disappoint. The writer of Psalm 42 knew this. We who are students of God's Word know it too. Regardless of the depth of our sorrow, we can embrace the sure and certain hope that God's perfect plan will prevail.

Are you staggering under the weight of a soul burden today? It's time to let it go. Surrender it to the One who's stronger than any three-time weight lifting champion. Let Him carry it for you.

"Why, my soul, are you downcast? Why so disturbed within me? Put your hope in God, for I will yet praise him, my Savior and my God" (v. 11).

Embrace the Truth: When soul-crushing trials enter my life, I can bring them to God and find hope.

Declare Your Faith: Lord, I believe I can find faith-sustaining hope in You, even when the circumstances of my life seem hopeless. Thank You for inspiring the writer of Psalm 42 so long ago to teach me how to deal with soul-crushing despair. Thank You too for the ability to believe even as I lament. Help me embrace the hope You offer and look forward to the day when the psalmist and I will praise You together for carrying us through. In the strong name of Jesus I pray, amen.

I believe . . .

God created the world with us in mind

[God] richly provides us with everything for our enjoyment.
1 Timothy 6:17

Do you remember your first day of school?

I can still picture my kindergarten classroom. I entered the room that morning to find a child-size desk with my name on it. The chair, too, was just the right size. For the first time, I didn't have to climb up onto a piece of furniture, nor did my feet dangle several inches above the floor. A newly sharpened purple pencil (my favorite color) waited for me in the well.

In a corner of the room, my teacher had created a reading nook. Soft pillows, a purple(!) shag rug, and a shelf full of age-appropriate books welcomed us. Comfortable heat hissed through the ancient radiators, knocking the chill from the September morning like a cozy cocoon. Mrs. DeMacy had gone to a lot of trouble to create the perfect environment for her beloved students.

Like my sweet kindergarten teacher, God the Father created the perfect environment for His beloved children.

Scientists tell us our world contains the perfect balance of everything necessary to support human life: "its distance from the sun . . . abundant liquid water, a breathable atmosphere, the perfectly sized sun to provide energy without killing life, and a perfectly sized moon to control the tides."[4]

But His creation didn't end with necessary-to-life elements. As sweet Mrs. DeMacy sought to create a functional *and* lovely space for her students to grow and learn, so God filled our world with custom details to touch the deepest parts of our lives. Stunning sunsets to dazzle our eyes. Lush nature to restore our souls. Delicious food to satisfy our hunger. And faithful companions to bring joy to our hearts.

Isaiah 6:3 captures the primary reason God created the world—to display His glory. "Holy, holy, holy is the Lord Almighty; the whole earth is full of his glory." But He also created the world to bring us joy. First Timothy 6:17 reminds us that God "richly provides us with everything for our enjoyment."

Embrace the Truth: God created our beautiful world with us in mind.

Declare Your Faith: Father, I can't get over the thought that when You were creating the world, You had us in mind. When You were planning the universe, You filled it with special touches we'd enjoy. I feel humbled and overwhelmed as I think about the love that guided Your creative hands. I love You so much, dear, kind Father.

I believe . . .

God can comfort others through me

Praise be to the God and Father of our Lord Jesus Christ, the Father of compassion and the God of all comfort, who comforts us in all our troubles, so that we can comfort those in any trouble with the comfort we ourselves receive from God.

2 Corinthians 1:3–4

There's nothing lonelier (or more terrifying) than waiting in a hospital for a report from your loved one's doctor. Years ago, a routine stress test revealed what looked like a life-threatening blockage in my husband's heart. "Go home, pack your bag, and return in the morning for a heart cath," the doctor said. "We may be doing open heart surgery."

The next day, I kissed my husband before they took him back and wondered if he'd have a six-inch scar down the middle of his chest the next time I saw him.

While I counted the minutes and watched for the doctor, I saw a familiar face.

"Ann Marie!"

"Lori! What are you doing here?"

"I could ask you the same thing."

When we swapped stories, I learned Ann Marie had been volunteering in the cardiac cath lab waiting room since her husband had passed away several years earlier. "I know how it feels to be waiting for test results," she said. "I sat in this room many times.

Now that Ray's gone, I want to help other families get through their own scary times."

My friend sat with me until the doctor arrived. "Your husband's heart looks just fine. As soon as he wakes up, you can see him." I hugged Ann Marie, and she moved on to the next family.

Ann Marie was living out 2 Corinthians 1:3–4, comforting others with the comfort she had received from God.

The apostle Paul wrote from experience as he encouraged the Corinthian believers not only to sympathize with those who were struggling but to comfort them. Because he'd suffered unimaginable trials as an apostle and received God's comfort, he had something to share with others walking through trials. So did the struggling Corinthians. And so do we.

"For just as we share abundantly in the sufferings of Christ, so also our comfort abounds through Christ" (v. 5).

Over the years, I've tried to follow Paul's—and Ann Marie's—example. I've reminded despairing parents that no child is so lost God cannot find them. I've shared with financially struggling friends how God provided for our family during times of sickness or unemployment. And I've wept with those who've lost loved ones and reminded them of the hope we have in Christ.

When we accept the comfort God tenderly offers, we heal. As we heal, we can see beyond ourselves to those around us who need a word of comfort. It's one way God redeems our suffering and uses it for good.

Embrace the Truth: When we receive the comfort God tenderly supplies, we can comfort others.

Declare Your Faith: Lord, I believe You can use the sorrows of my life to help ease the sufferings of others. Thank You for wrapping me in a blanket of comfort big enough to cover a world of hurting people. Lift my eyes from my sorrow and help me see others who need the hope and help that's only found in You. In Jesus's name I pray, amen.

I believe . . .

God calls believers to unity in Christ

That they may be one as we are one—I in them and you in me—so that they may be brought to complete unity.
John 17:22–23

"We considered driving away," Wilbur said with a shrug. "We were afraid we were in trouble or about to get run off, but we stayed to see what they'd say."

The teenagers sat up straighter in their seats as two Black men approached their car.

It was the 1950s in rural South Carolina. Not yet turbulent but characterized by clear racial boundaries that had been in place for centuries.

Now Wilbur and his friend Pinson had stepped over one.

Sunday in the South meant two things for the boys—church and Wilbur's sister Leila's fried chicken. They'd already been to the small church Wilbur's family attended each week. Pinson, sixteen years old and proud of his new driver's license, was eager to show off his skills. And hoping to be invited to dinner.

"Want me to give you a ride home?" he'd asked Wilbur after church.

The sun glinted off the shiny chrome as Pinson maneuvered the family's Plymouth off the main road. The scent of warm earth drew their eyes to a farmer's newly tilled field. Across the street sat a white cinderblock building with a simple cross.

As they slowed to make the turn, the sound of a tambourine

reached their ears. And then another. Pinson glanced at Wilbur and raised an eyebrow. Wilbur responded with two raised eyebrows and a nod. Pinson eased the car onto the edge of the property and cut the engine.

Music unlike anything they'd ever heard in their church bounced out of the open windows. Voices rose and fell in waves. Feet stomped, and hands clapped in time with the music.

"Hallelujah!" one voice said.

"Thank You, Jesus," another responded.

How long the boys sat there as the joyful sounds embraced them, neither could tell. "Swing Low, Sweet Chariot" flowed seamlessly into "Down by the Riverside," which eased into "Gonna Shout All Over God's Heaven."

But their grins faded as two men emerged from the church and made their way toward them.

"Should we leave?" Pinson whispered.

"Let's see what they have to say."

"What you boys doin' here?" A tall man in a bow tie and a blazer asked.

"Listenin'," Wilbur said, his voice higher than normal. "We're enjoying your worship."

Bowtie man raised his eyebrow and looked over the car roof at his companion. The man raised two eyebrows and nodded his head toward the church.

"You can hear better from inside," the first man said. "Care to join us?"

Wilbur and Pinson exchanged glances.

"Sure!" they said, scrambling for the door handles.

Wilbur may have felt like the apostle Peter did as he worshiped with the gentiles of Cornelius's house—so different from himself in race, culture, and upbringing—yet so full of faith and the Holy Spirit.

"I now realize how true it is," Peter said, "that God does not show favoritism but accepts from every nation the one who fears him and does what is right" (Acts 10:34–35).

Did Peter understand he was seeing the fulfillment of what Jesus had asked God for so earnestly on the night He was betrayed: "That they may be one as we are one—I in them and you in me—so that they may be brought to complete unity" (John 17:22–23)?

Seventy years later, Wilbur still smiles at the memory. "We weren't Black or White. Just Christians worshiping the Lord together."

Embrace the Truth: God calls believers to unity in Christ.

Declare Your Faith: Lord, thank You that Your death on the cross tore down the dividing wall between races, cultures, and peoples. Help us live in light of this. I believe You will draw people to Yourself when we set aside our differences and embrace the unity we have in Christ. Use us to help others find the unity that comes from having You as our Father.

I believe . . .

God's mercy never ends

The steadfast love of the Lord never ceases;
his mercies never come to an end.
Lamentations 3:22 ESV

Seventy-six thousand, six hundred and fifty. If we live to be seventy years old and commit three sins a day, we'll have committed 76,650 sins by the end of our lifetime.

You may take exception to this. I did, the first time I heard it. What Christian commits seventy-six thousand sins?

The number is staggering, but I suspect it represents only a fraction of the sins we commit in our lifetime. Think about it. A sin is anything we do that breaks God's law, everything we *don't* do that we should, and everything we think about that we shouldn't—anger, jealousy, selfish ambition, hatred. Only three sins a day? More like three sins an hour. On bad days, maybe three sins a minute.

Most Christians want to live a life that honors God, but we wrestle with our propensity to sin.

This is why I'm forever grateful for God's unending mercy.

Jeremiah declared in Lamentations 3:22, "The steadfast love of the Lord never ceases; his mercies never come to an end" (ESV).

What makes this declaration so powerful is that it came during one of the darkest times in Judah's history. For centuries God's people had sinned against Him. They offered their children in the fire to false gods, committed perverted sexual acts of worship to idols, and turned their backs on the one true God.

In love, God judged their sin by sending the Assyrians to

conquer their land and carry them off to Babylon. Yet in the midst of His judgment, God reminded them of His unfailing love and His endless mercies.

The Jews needed to remember that God's love is steadfast, and so do we. On our good days and our bad days, God loves us. He'll correct us when we sin, but He'll never stop loving us.

We also need to remember that God's mercies never end. As sinful people, we deserve His eternal wrath. Instead He offers us eternal forgiveness and a relationship with Him through Jesus Christ. Even when He allows us to suffer the consequences of our sinful actions, He grants us the mercy of an irrevocable pardon because Jesus paid our sin debt. True believers need not fear eternal punishment.

If you're having a good day, perhaps you aren't thinking much about God's mercy. It might be good to consider the more than 76,650 sins you'll accumulate over your lifetime and thank Him for His mercy.

If you're having a bad day, you might wonder if God's going to give up on you. Confess and forsake your sin—again; accept His gift of never-ending mercy; and ask Him to transform you.

"Because of his great love for us, God, *who is rich in mercy*, made us alive with Christ even when we were dead in transgressions—it is by grace you have been saved" (Ephesians 2:4–5, emphasis added).

Embrace the Truth: God's never-ending mercy is vast enough to atone for every sin I'll ever commit.

Declare Your Faith: Lord, I believe You lavish Your mercy on me. I can't earn it, and I'll never deserve it, but oh, how grateful I am. I never want to take sin lightly. When I sin, help me come to You for mercy and forgiveness. I love You, Lord. Amen.

I believe . . .

I can have peace

You keep him in perfect peace whose mind is
stayed on you, because he trusts in you.

Isaiah 26:3 ESV

Had you watched my husband and me walk from the elevator to the ship's dining room on the last night of our cruise, you'd have bet your souvenir money I'd been hanging out at the Blue Iguana bar. A fierce storm churned up the Caribbean waters and tossed our ship like a sock in a front-loading washer. The waves were so high they splashed against the windows in the dining room seven decks above sea level.

As the ship pitched and rolled, I struggled to maintain my balance. At one point, the floor seemed to drop beneath my feet, and I instinctively reached for my husband's arm. His steady presence anchored me and enabled me to walk the remaining fifty feet to our table.

That was my first storm at sea, but I've experienced quite a few storms in my soul.

Have you?

There we are, sailing along, enjoying the sunshine, and suddenly, life grows dark. Clouds of sickness or financial challenge appear on the horizon. The waters of marital, family, or church relationships grow choppy. The winds of change or loss blow hard across our life. The sunshine vanishes, and a gale begins.

Thankfully, drowning isn't our only option when we find ourselves in the midst of a figurative nor'easter. We can navigate storms with peace instead of panic. The prophet Isaiah shows us how. "You keep him in perfect peace whose mind is stayed on you, because he trusts in you" (Isaiah 26:3 ESV).

These Holy Spirit–inspired words assure us we'll have peace when our minds are "stayed on" God.

What does it mean to be stayed on God?

The Hebrew word for "stayed on" is *samak*. It means to lean upon something reflexively. During the storm at sea, my first response was to reach out to my husband and lean on him for support. When life storms threaten to swamp us, we should do the same with God. Crying out to Him for wisdom, protection, provision, or healing should be our first response, not our last. I call this "spiritual muscle memory."

How do we develop spiritual muscle memory? By training.

I'm confident that if our cruise ship had been in real danger, the crew would have responded with appropriate lifesaving measures. They didn't learn those measures by reading the safety manual the morning we sailed. They practiced them over and over long before the first passenger stepped on board.

The same is true for us. As we learn God's character through the disciplines of prayer and Bible reading, when a crisis enters our life, our default setting, our *super*natural response, will be to reach out to God and *samak*—lean on Him.

As we do, His steady presence will anchor our minds and enable us to walk in faith. Instead of drowning in the waves, His perfect peace will quiet the storm in our heart.

Embrace the Truth: Leaning on God keeps me in perfect peace—even in life's fiercest storms.

Declare Your Faith: Lord, I believe I can have peace even when my life is in turmoil. I confess that sometimes, oftentimes, my first response is to lean on myself, not on You, but I don't want to do this anymore. Help me seek You through Bible reading and prayer so my understanding of You will grow, and so will my spiritual muscle memory. I long for the peace that comes from fully trusting You. In the strong name of Jesus I pray, amen.

I believe . . .

God created me as I am for a purpose

We are his workmanship, created in Christ Jesus for good works, which God prepared beforehand, that we should walk in them.

Ephesians 2:10 ESV

"What's he making?" my daughter asked as we watched the artisan breathe into a metal pipe with a lump of molten glass at the end. Another breath, and the glob stretched and thinned.

"A Christmas ornament?" I guessed. He blew again. "Nope. Too big."

"Maybe a bowl," she said.

The man turned and set the orb onto a table, gently pressing until the bottom was flat. Guiding the still soft glass with his tools, he stretched and shaped it. A pinch at the top formed a spout. When he added a handle, we knew.

"A pitcher," my daughter declared, delighted she'd solved the mystery.

We turned from the window that separated the craftsman's workspace from his shop. Dozens of pieces filled the shelves—pitchers, bowls, dishes, glassware, Christmas ornaments, home décor, and serving pieces. Each work of art had a different function, but all bore the distinctive touch of the artist.

The apostle Paul described a similar display of craftsmanship when he wrote about the church, God's body of believers—us. "We are his workmanship," he said.

Workmanship by definition implies a worker, a plan, and a purpose. Our existence isn't a random happening or part of the ebb and flow of nature. We were "created in Christ Jesus for good works, which God prepared beforehand, that we should walk in them" (Ephesians 2:10 ESV).

My daughter and I watched as the glassblower fashioned each of his articles based on the purpose he intended it for. He put a handle on a pitcher so someone could use it to carry water. He made a bowl with high sides so someone could fill it with food. He put a loop on a Christmas ornament so someone could hang it on a tree. But he didn't put a loop on a pitcher or give an ornament high sides or a handle.

God created us exactly as He did, uniquely, because He has a specific purpose for each of us. Some He created to be pitchers to carry living water across the seas to spiritually thirsty people. Others He created to be bowls to feed the hungry. Still others He created to be ornaments to display His mercy and grace.

We can trust that God made us as He did to equip us for the good works He prepared beforehand for us to do.

When we surrender ourselves to God just as we are, we're free to ask Him how best to use the way He made us for His kingdom and glory.

Embrace the Truth: God created us—just as we are—for the good works He prepared for us to do.

Declare Your Faith: Lord, I believe You uniquely created me because You have good works planned for me to do. I'll be honest, though. Sometimes, when I look at how You made me, I wonder what You were thinking. But I choose to trust that You knew what You were doing. Help me surrender myself to You, to be used for Your good purposes, even when I can't imagine how You're going to do it. Amen.

I believe . . .

My labor isn't in vain

My dear brothers and sisters, stand firm. Let nothing move you. Always give yourselves fully to the work of the Lord, because you know that your labor in the Lord is not in vain.

1 Corinthians 15:58

"I don't know if I can ever go back into the country," Mariana said. She lifted her eyes to meet mine, but I could tell her thoughts were far away. "All that work. All those years. All those relationships." Her voice rose in frustration, then ended in a sigh. "An entire ministry gone with one swoop of an evil dictator's pen." She shook her head, and the tear that had shimmered in the corner of her eye escaped and slid down her cheek. "It looked so promising . . ."

I've never been kicked out of a foreign country, but I've experienced the heartbreak of a closed door. I suspect you have too. A friendship ends. A ministry season concludes. The invitation you hoped for didn't come, and now you're feeling rejected and confused. "I wanted to serve You, Lord," you pray. "Wasn't I good enough?"

The apostle Paul, writing to the struggling church at Corinth, spent fifteen out of sixteen chapters encouraging, exhorting, and rebuking the disciples. He counseled them as a father would his children—with tough love and a tender heart. He spoke words of hope over their future and described heaven and Christ's triumph over sin, hell, and death.

Near the end of his letter, he penned words that lifted their drooping shoulders and strengthened their doubting hearts. "My dear brothers and sisters, stand firm. Let nothing move you. Always give yourselves fully to the work of the Lord, because you know that your labor in the Lord is not in vain" (1 Corinthians 15:58).

Your labor in the Lord is not in vain.

Paul declared what history has proven—that no word of God falls to the ground. No deed done in faith escapes His notice. God not only sees it but He uses it to advance His kingdom—whether or not we see results. Nothing done in the name of Jesus is wasted.

Do you believe this?

Mariana does. After she grieved the ministry that was no more, she continued to serve God. Today she ministers in her local church to people of the same nationality she worked with overseas. The experience she gained in her ten years abroad helps her minister to and identify with that people group in ways other volunteers can't.

Mariana still mourns the work and people she left behind, but she's chosen to give herself fully to the work of the Lord—however and wherever God opens a door. She knows by faith that her labor in the Lord is not in vain.

Embrace the Truth: Nothing done with a sincere heart in Jesus's name is wasted.

Declare Your Faith: Lord, I believe nothing I've done for You is wasted. Though doubts sometimes niggle at my heart, I choose to believe by faith that You'll use everything I've done in Your name for others' good and Your glory. Help me stand firm in You when doors close or I don't see the results I hoped for. In Jesus's name I pray, amen.

I believe . . .

I'm never alone

Where can I go from your Spirit? Where can I flee from your presence?
Psalm 139:7

If I asked you to describe a time when you felt incredibly alone—not just absent from people but separated in mind, body, and spirit from anyone who cared about you—what would you say?

I experienced this type of aloneness in the Narita airport in Tokyo. I'd traveled from Columbia, South Carolina, to Yokosuka, Japan, to visit my daughter. After ten fun-filled days, she drove me an hour away to catch my flight home. We hugged goodbye, then hugged again. After a final squeeze, I watched her taillights disappear into a sea of cars.

All went well—until it didn't. After the plane (with me on it) sat on the tarmac for thirty minutes, the captain announced they had "a slight mechanical problem." Slight or serious, we were getting ready to fly fourteen hours over the Pacific Ocean and Alaska. Take all the time you need, I thought.

As the minutes passed, "Remain seated with your seat belts fastened," became, "You may unbuckle and move freely about the cabin," which became, "We're allowing you to deplane—and please take your belongings with you."

In the terminal, I couldn't connect to the airport's Wi-Fi, and my phone's SIM card didn't allow me to make calls. I had no way to let my husband know I'd be delayed. By now my daughter was home and in bed. She wouldn't suspect anything was amiss until late the next day, when I failed to arrive home.

As I pondered my predicament, tears sprang to my eyes. Seven thousand miles from home and surrounded by a crush of people speaking languages I couldn't understand, a deep sense of aloneness settled over me.

David the shepherd never flew to Japan, but he also experienced a profound sense of loneliness. While I was safe in a relatively comfortable airport, he was forced to flee from the murderous King Saul. He left behind everyone he loved and struck out for the desert. He moved constantly, sleeping in caves and clefts of the rock. God had promised to make him king, yet for years he lived as a fugitive. "Turn to me and be gracious to me," he prayed in Psalm 25:16, "for I am lonely and afflicted."

Stripped of the security of home, family, and friends, David turned to the One who had promised never to leave or forsake him. "Hear my voice when I call, LORD," he prayed. "Be merciful to me and answer me" (Psalm 27:7). In response to his prayer, David received sweet confirmation of God's presence. "Though my father and mother forsake me," he declared, "the LORD will receive me" (v. 10).

God spoke to my heart: "Where can you go from my Spirit? Where can you flee from my presence? If you go up to the heavens, I'm there; if you make your bed in the depths, I'm there. If you rise on the wings of the dawn, if you settle on the far side of the sea, even there my hand will guide you, my right hand will hold you fast" (Psalm 139:7–10, personalized).

David wasn't alone in the caves of Adullam, and I wasn't alone in the airport in Narita. We're not alone in doctor's offices, unemployment lines, or at home. God walks with us through the loneliness of divorce, disease, and disappointment. He is nearer than a whisper and as close as a prayer. He holds us when we sleep, and when we awaken He is with us. God was with David the shepherd, and He was with me.

It took a few hours, but the mechanics made the repairs, and my plane departed. I awakened with the coastline of California in view and the words of John Newton's beloved hymn rising in my heart: "'Tis grace has brought me safe thus far, and grace will lead me home."

Embrace the Truth: No matter where we go, we never leave God's presence. He is always with us.

Declare Your Faith: Lord, I believe, as the psalmist wrote, that You surround me with Your presence. You've promised to never leave me nor forsake me, so I may boldly say, "The Lord is my helper. Of whom shall I be afraid?" (Hebrews 13:6). Sometimes, though, I forget this. I grow frightened and feel alone. When this happens, remind me You are as close as a prayer. I love You, kind Father. Amen.

I believe . . .

I can be bold

Grant to your servants to continue to
speak your word with all boldness.
Acts 4:29 ESV

After Allie surrendered her life to Christ at age twelve, she looked at the world through fresh eyes. Instead of seeing people as old, young, friendly, or standoffish, she realized there were only two types: saved and lost.

"Does Mrs. Sanders know Jesus?" she asked her mom one day. "She seems pretty grumpy."

"I don't think so, honey. She told me once she used to go to church when her husband was alive, but now she doesn't 'believe in that stuff anymore.'"

"That's sad." Allie said. "She must be very lonely."

From that day on, normally shy Allie attempted to befriend her crusty next-door neighbor. She "happened" to meet Mrs. Sanders at their adjoining mailboxes. She asked about her dog and told her about school. One day, Allie brought over fresh-baked cookies and an invitation to dinner with her family. Before long, Mrs. Sanders became a regular guest at their Saturday night suppers. Allie invited her to church, but the woman always refused.

"Mrs. Sanders," Allie said one Saturday night three years into the friendship. "My youth choir is singing during the Easter service tomorrow. I sure would love it if you'd come hear us."

Mrs. Sanders shocked everyone by saying, "I think I'd like that."

To Allie's delight, Mrs. Sanders met them in the driveway the next morning. After service, over an Easter feast of ham, deviled eggs, and sweet potato casserole, she asked Allie's mother which Bible version they used. "I need a new one," she said. "I want to read it again."

I wouldn't ordinarily have chosen the word *bold* to describe Allie, but she was bold in her concern for Mrs. Sanders. She reminds me of two other Christ followers, Peter and John.

Acts 4 describes how the men courageously proclaimed Jesus before the most powerful Jewish leaders. The result? "When they saw the boldness of Peter and John, and perceived that they were uneducated, common men, they were astonished. And they recognized that they had been with Jesus" (v. 13 ESV).

Afterward, as the disciples submitted the authorities' threats to God in prayer, "the place in which they were gathered together was shaken, and they were all filled with the Holy Spirit and continued to speak the word of God with boldness" (v. 31). After they were jailed, instead of asking God to shield them from the authorities or protect them from punishment, they asked God to "grant to your servants to continue to speak your word with all boldness" (v. 29 ESV). God answered, and the disciples fearlessly proclaimed the gospel wherever they went.

Few of us will have the opportunity to proclaim Christ to powerful and influential people, although some might. But God often gives us "ordinary" chances to speak in His name.

We can boldly defend the unborn, the overlooked, and the oppressed. We can courageously share our faith with our family members, often the scariest people to witness to. And we can zealously push back against today's anti-God culture through our testimony, our loving acts, and our countercultural, Christlike character.

Sometimes being bold for Jesus means sharing the gospel with thousands, as Peter and John did. Other times it means reaching out to one lonely soul, as Allie did with her neighbor. Whatever our assignment, the Holy Spirit and the hope of the gospel will empower us.

"Since we have such a hope," Paul wrote, "we are very bold" (2 Corinthians 3:12).

Embrace the Truth: By the power of the Holy Spirit, we can boldly declare the truth of God, even when we're afraid.

Declare Your Faith: Lord, I believe I can speak boldly in Jesus's name through the power of Your Holy Spirit, who lives in me. I confess I often allow fear to silence me. Enable me to step out in faith and open my mouth to share boldly the hope I have in Christ. Make me aware of those around me who need to talk with someone who's been with Jesus. Amen.

I believe . . .

Jesus is my friend

. . . a friend of tax collectors and sinners.

Matthew 11:19

Linda was my first real friend. When we were six, we shared a set of front steps (and more than a few popsicles). We played Barbies, spent the night together, and talked about everything. We were besties.

One day, feeling especially trusting, I shared the deepest, darkest secret of my young life.

"I still suck my thumb at bedtime."

Linda blinked, thought a moment, then shrugged. "It's okay. I still like you."

I released the breath I'd been holding. Basking in the warmth of her unconditional love, I grinned. "You're my best friend."

Not all my friends have been as accepting—or as close—as Linda. As I've aged, my secrets have grown deeper and my insecurities have multiplied. What will this friend think of me if I tell her I'm struggling in my marriage, my parenting, or my faith? Will she still like me once she gets to know me? Can I trust her with the personal parts of my life, or should I keep things superficial?

God created us to live in community, and we're blessed if we experience true human friendship on this side of eternity. But even if we don't, Jesus will always be our friend.

"I have called you friends," Jesus told His disciples, "for everything that I learned from my Father I have made known to you" (John 15:15).

More deeply than any other friend, Jesus shared His heart with

His disciples. They knew what made Him laugh and what made Him cry. What made Him angry and what amazed Him. We can know this too, because He reveals it to us through the Holy Spirit and God's Word. Jesus doesn't have to let us into His heart and mind, but, wonder of wonder, He does—every day if we seek Him.

Because He's our friend, He offers us His committed love. And He calls us to offer Him ours. Even as a six-year-old, I knew my friendship with Linda required loyalty and love. Our friendship with Jesus, our Savior and the lover of our soul, deserves this and more.

Jesus is the friend of sinners—of me and of you. Aren't we glad He is?

Embrace the Truth: Jesus offers us friendship and committed love. He deserves the same from us.

Declare Your Faith: Lord, I believe You are my friend. Wow. Despite all my failures, You love me. You share Your heart with me whenever I draw near. Help me love You with the loyalty and commitment You deserve. When I grieve You with my sin, convict me, so I can confess and forsake it quickly. Better yet, help me not sin against You at all. Give me the same type of pure love for You that You have for me. Amen.

I believe . . .

Our suffering will end

I consider that our present sufferings are not worth comparing with the glory that will be revealed in us.
Romans 8:18

"My captors said if I revealed the names of my missionary co-workers, they'd go easy on me. If I didn't, every day they'd cut off one of my fingers."

It was the third day of our missions conference, and my husband, David, had asked Raul to speak to our youth group.

As he told his story, silence descended on the room. No shuffling feet. No whispered comments. Just silence. And Raul's voice.

"We were ministering in a Muslim country, and several of our neighbors had come to faith in Christ. Then someone turned us in. The police burst into my apartment and took me away."

Raul took a deep breath, eyes closed to the memory.

"In the morning, they interrogated me."

He paused for a moment and looked around at the youths hanging on his words. He placed his hands on the table and extended his fingers—his nine remaining fingers.

"I felt nothing when they chopped off my finger, but it hurt like crazy afterward. But I was still alive—and so were my teammates."

Several of the teens stared. Others looked away.

"The next day, they released me. I have no idea why."

Tears shimmered in his eyes as he held up his four-fingered hand. "This is my badge of honor. I consider it a small price to pay for the One who gave so much for me."

I pray none of us will ever lose a finger for the sake of Christ, but all Christians suffer somehow.

A spouse, family member, or coworker torments us because of our faith. We suffer loss—perhaps a job, a friend, or a relationship—because of our commitment to Christ. We may even go to jail.

Sometimes we don't suffer *for* Christ, but we suffer *in* Christ. In a broken world surrounded by broken people, their brokenness becomes our pain. Grief, financial challenges, sickness, and turbulent relationships mar the beauty of our lives. We agonize in prayer—for years—over our beloved prodigals.

Will we wear our hardships as a badge of honor and consider them a small price to pay for the One who gave so much for us?

That trying season fraught with health challenges? A thread in the tapestry of forever.

A lifetime of laboring in faith for our spouse, our child, our job, or our ministry? A twinkle eclipsed by the blazing glow of eternity.

Years of praying, hoping, witnessing, and believing? A raindrop in the ocean of heaven.

One second after we take our last breath here, the trials of this life will fade away, and God will wipe the tears from our eyes. "Well done, good and faithful servant! You have been faithful with a few things; I will put you in charge of many things. Come and share your master's happiness!" (Matthew 25:21).

As we stand before Him free from sin and struggle, God will fling open the heavenly doors and welcome us into our forever home.

When I get to that heavenly banquet hall, I hope to sit next to Raul. Maybe we'll exchange a high five—not a high four—as we marvel at what God has done.

"Weeping may tarry for the night," the psalmist declared, "but joy comes with the morning" (Psalm 30:5 ESV).

And in heaven, morning will last forever.

Embrace the Truth: Our suffering will end, but our joy-filled eternity will last forever.

Declare Your Faith: Lord, I believe that one day any suffering I've experienced on this earth will vanish, and I'll live with You forever in heaven. I can't wait for when I can hand You my sorrow and You'll exchange it for joy. Thank You, Father, for the promise of heaven.

I believe . . .

Every day is Good Morning

This is the day that the LORD has made;
let us rejoice and be glad in it.
Psalm 118:24 ESV

I sat in my daughter's darkened living room, hoping for an hour of quiet before my four grandchildren awakened. Work commitments had called Mary Leigh and her husband away from home hours before dawn. I'd agreed to sit with the children until she returned.

Resting my head on the back of the couch, I mentally scrolled through the day ahead. A full schedule of dental patients. An article to edit on my lunch hour. A mad dash home to fix dinner, then out again for a writer's meeting. If the meeting didn't run long, I'd return home in time to make lunches for tomorrow and fall into bed. I sighed.

Maybe I could catch a few more minutes of sleep.

Tap. Tap. Tap. Shuffle. Shuffle. Tap. Tap.

"Hi, Gigi! What you doin' here?"

I opened my eyes to see Collin, the almost-four-year-old, standing before me, barely visible in the darkness. He'd crawled from bed hoping for a bagel or bowl of cereal. Instead, he'd found his Gigi lounging on the sofa.

I reached for him and drew him close. We sat there for a long while, talking about frogs, the scrape on his knee, and his newest stuffie.

Suddenly, he sat up and pointed to the window where the morning sun was peeking through the blinds.

"Look, Gigi," he exclaimed. "It's Good Morning!"

I laughed at his clever phrasing and his delight. "You're right, Collin. It *is* Good Morning."

Sometimes, when the cares of life weigh heavily, I need to be reminded that every morning is good.

"This is the day that the Lord has made," the psalmist wrote. "Let us rejoice and be glad in it" (Psalm 118:24 esv).

This is the day. We can rejoice in yesterday, when life was easier and troubles few. We can rejoice in tomorrow, when trials might lift and circumstances improve. But *this* day—the one the Lord has made for our good and His glory—should be the object of our joy.

What is our proper response to each day He gives us? "Let us rejoice and be glad in it."

But how? Why should we rejoice when *this day* is hard? Sad? Overwhelming? Lonely?

The psalmist provides at least four reasons:

We can rejoice because God is good (v. 1). We need never suspect His motives, wonder about His reasons, or question His character. He is good, and everything He allows into our lives will be for our good. Because He cannot act outside His nature, everything that touches us will accomplish good, if not in this world, then in the next (Romans 8:28).

We can rejoice because God's steadfast love endures forever (Psalm 118:1). It marches through time on a relentless quest to call lost sinners to salvation. It draws us, shelters us, and keeps us. God's love never fails.

We can rejoice because the Lord is on our side (vv. 6–7). When we walk in integrity and stand for truth, God stands beside us. He defends and protects us. He walks with us through even the valley of the shadow of death and helps us fear no evil (Psalm 23:4).

Finally, we can rejoice because we "shall not die, but . . . live, and recount the deeds of the Lord" (v. 17). Whether God spares our life in a near accident, heals us from a life-threatening disease, or takes us home to be with Him, we shall not die. In this life and in the next, we'll live in His presence and "recount the deeds of the LORD" forever.

Whether you're anticipating the day ahead or dreading it, I invite you to consider Psalm 118 and declare with Collin, "It's Good Morning!"

Embrace the Truth: When we know the Lord, every day is Good Morning.

Declare Your Faith: Lord, I believe every day is good, even when the events of that day are anything but good. While I can't always change my circumstances, I can change my thoughts about them. Today—and every day, with Your help—I'll embrace the time You've given me and praise You for it. "You are my God, and I will give thanks to you; you are my God; I will extol you. Oh give thanks to the LORD, for he is good; for his steadfast love endures forever!" (Psalm 118:28–29 ESV).

I believe . . .

God is always at work

Jesus said to them, "My Father is always at his work to this very day, and I too am working."
John 5:17

"I did my best to raise Tommy in the faith," Maddie said to our prayer group. "We prayed together, read Bible stories every night at bedtime . . ." Her voice trailed off. "Something changed around fourteen. All of a sudden it wasn't cool to love Jesus. He still went to church—we made him go—but he ditched his church friends and started hanging around with troublemakers."

"It was a very long ten years." Her friend Jen, sitting beside her, nodded at the memory. Maddie continued, "Lying, drinking, sneaking out. When he went off to college, we thought he might turn things around, but he didn't. He dropped out of school and started working at a gym. Sleeping on friends' couches. We only heard from him when he needed money."

She looked around the circle of women. "I prayed so much for him, but nothing changed."

Suddenly a smile crept into her eyes. "Or so I thought."

"One day he called me—out of the blue. 'Mom,' he said, 'I got saved. And I'm getting baptized on Sunday. I want you and Dad to be there.'"

Maddie put her hand over her heart as she described the phone call. "At first I couldn't speak. Then I asked him, 'What happened?'"

"'I woke up one day, hungover from the night before,' he said. 'My head was about to explode, and I was sick to my stomach. I heard this voice in my head: *You don't have to live this way.*

"'I knew it was God. He was talking to me. "God," I said, "I can't do this alone. You gotta help me." And He has. I told Him I was sorry for the things I've done and that I wanted Him to be in control of my life. I've been going to church too. Making new friends. And I'm getting baptized on Sunday.'"

Maddie paused. One woman sniffled. Another wiped her eyes. "I had no idea any of this was going on. All those years, I felt so hopeless. Why weren't my prayers working?"

I wonder if the man lying paralyzed at the pool of Bethesda felt the same way. Did God hear his prayers? If He did, why didn't He answer them?

Maddie didn't know God was at work in her son's life. The paralyzed man didn't know God was at work in his. As a five-year-old boy, he didn't know God had already sent His Son, Jesus, into the world. He didn't know, as he languished on his mat, that God was setting the stage for one of Jesus's greatest miracles. And he didn't know, when the time was right, that God would answer his thirty-eight years of prayer with eight simple words. "Get up! Pick up your mat and walk" (John 5:8).

"My Father is always at his work to this very day," Jesus said, "and I too am working" (v. 17). Even when we can't see Him. When we pray and nothing happens. When hearts grow cold and circumstances seem hopeless.

God is always at work.

Always.

Embrace the Truth: Even when I can't see any evidence, I know God is always at work.

Declare Your Faith: Lord, I believe You are always at work in the world around me. Because Jesus said You were, even when I can't see any evidence of it, I choose to trust that this is true. Give me faith to believe You can do exceedingly, abundantly above all I could ever ask or imagine. Amen.

I believe . . .

I can glorify God in my death

Jesus said this to indicate the kind of death
by which Peter would glorify God.
John 21:19

I always thought it was morbid when people talked about dying. Death was the last thing I wanted to think about. I was young, strong, and healthy. Death seemed far away. And, truth be told, I superstitiously feared if I talked about it, it might happen.

Now that I'm officially not young anymore, I sometimes wonder how I'll leave this earth. My first choice, probably yours as well, is for Jesus to return and call us all home together. How amazing would that be? Even so, come quickly, Lord Jesus.

Dying in my sleep at 103, in full command of my mind and body, after living a productive and healthy life, comes in a close second. But I've lived long enough to realize that God grants this option to a rare few.

The rest of us will probably have to walk the valley of the shadow of death. And the shadows are many. Debilitating disease, accidents, and other life-ending circumstances top the list.

God allowed Peter to die as a martyr. And, unlike most of us, Peter knew well in advance how it would happen. On the shores of Galilee, after a breakfast of roasted fish, Jesus gave him a glimpse of his death: "When you are old you will stretch out your hands, and someone else will dress you and lead you where you do not want to go" (John 21:18). History fills in the details: Peter was arrested and crucified upside down, at his request, because he felt unworthy to die as his Savior had.

"Jesus said this," John wrote, "to indicate the kind of death by which Peter would glorify God" (v. 19). Did you catch that? The kind of death by which Peter would *glorify God.*

Have you ever considered that your own death could glorify God? Me neither—until I read this Scripture passage. And until I watched believer after suffering believer *glorify God* while dying.

Linda grew sweeter and more bold to share the reason for her hope as she experienced the effects of MS. Mary spent the days of her last hospital stay phoning friends, relatives, and coworkers, righting a lifetime of wrongs. Frank, who often couldn't sleep because of chronic back pain, spent his sleepless nights praying for his family and friends.

Ninety-year-old Grace bore the indignities of her ever-increasing frailty with faith and, well, grace. She grew sweeter, not grumpier, as her health declined. She took every opportunity to thank her family, doctors, and caregivers. On days she felt too weak to leave her bed, she prayed and meditated on Scripture. She sent cards to members of her church, encouraging them in their faith. She mentored younger women from her recliner. When visitors came to encourage her, she encouraged them.

My friend and writing mentor, Sue, agonizing under the ravages of pancreatic cancer, wrote about how God met her in the darkness of her hospital room and shared visions of hope and heaven.

We don't know when or how we'll die. We do know that unless Jesus returns, we'll one day walk the valley of the shadow of death. Let's decide now, with Peter, Linda, Mary, Frank, Grace, and Sue, to glorify God in our lives—and in our deaths.

Embrace the Truth: Even in death, I can glorify God.

Declare Your Faith: Lord, I believe I can bring glory to You by the way I die. I want this to be my last act of worship and service to You. I don't know the details of my demise, but however You choose for me to leave this earth, I want to die well—full of faith, winsome in my witness, and powerful in courage and trust. The thought of dying is scary, but I trust You to walk with me every step of the way. Equip me with everything I need to glorify You all the days of my life—and in my death. I love You. Amen.

I believe . . .

God answers prayer

The prayer of a righteous person is powerful and effective.
James 5:16

At the Christian college where David went to school, Friday night was basketball night. Students gathered from all over campus to cheer for their team and enjoy each other's company. Usually, David was right there in the middle of the action. But not that semester.

Motivated by a story one of his professors had shared, he and his roommate had committed to spend every Friday night in the chapel, praying for the wives they didn't have yet.

"You may not know who your future spouse is," the prof had said, "but they're in the world somewhere. They need you to pray for them. Pray for their safety. Pray for their purity. Pray for their salvation."

So pray they did. Every Friday night until the semester ended. Nothing changed as far as David could tell. No bride dropped out of the sky. But he assumed God had heard his prayers.

Three hundred miles away, a senior in high school was having the worst semester of her life. Despite being one of the top students in her class, earning a full tuition scholarship to the college of her choice, and dating a boy everyone assumed she'd someday marry, she was miserable.

As the semester drew to a close, she grew more and more fearful. She knew the decisions she was making would chart the course of her life, and she felt woefully inadequate to make them. Desperate, she sought help from her pastor and surrendered her life to Christ.

Two years later, she met David. They fell in love and married a year later.

One night, David and his bride were talking about their spiritual journeys and marveling at how God had saved them.

"What year did you commit your life to Christ?" David asked her. When she answered, he counted back—all the way back to that semester when he and his roommate had skipped basketball games to pray for the wives they didn't have yet.

When he told his wife the story—and the timing—they wept grateful tears. God overwhelmed them by how He moves His children to pray and then works through their prayers.

David doesn't always receive quick answers to his prayers. He prayed for twenty-six years before his brother surrendered his life to Christ. He's still praying for some family members and friends. However long it takes, he knows God hears, and he trusts Him to answer according to His perfect will and timing.

When he forgets, David looks at his wife, and God reminds him that "the prayer of a righteous person is powerful and effective" (James 5:16).

God reminds me too, because I am that wife.

Embrace the Truth: In His perfect will and timing, God answers the prayers of His children.

Declare Your Faith: Lord, I believe You answer prayer. Even when I don't see answers, or when You answer differently than I'd hoped, I believe You respond to every one of my requests. Thank You that the righteousness that grants me the right to pray to You is not my own but Christ's. Help me bring every need to You and trust You to do what is best. In the strong name of Jesus I pray, amen.

I believe . . .

God will guide me through life

Show me your ways, LORD, teach me your paths.
Guide me in your truth and teach me, for you are God
my Savior, and my hope is in you all day long.
Psalm 25:4–5

Three hubcaps. My husband, David, bought me three hubcaps in one year. Some wives get flowers. I get hubcaps.

"I don't understand why they keep falling off," I wailed when he discovered yet another hubcap missing from my car. "I haven't hit a curb in a long time."

The next time he drove with me, he voiced his suspicion. "Potholes. You've hit two in the short time we've been driving. This could be what's making your hubcaps fall off. Try to drive around them."

"I'll try," I said, "but most of the time I don't see them until it's too late."

A few days later I was following David home from church. We'd come from our workplaces and had driven separate cars. As I drove behind him, I saw him swerve, so I followed his lead. I expected to see a squished squirrel or a tree branch in the road. Instead, I saw—you guessed it—a pothole. A few miles later, he swerved again, and so did I.

"If I could follow you around all day," I said when we arrived home, "I'd never hit another pothole. And I'd never lose another hubcap."

Unfortunately, my husband can't lead me through every pothole-filled street, but I have an even better guide. One who will lead me in paths of righteousness and steer me around the potholes of sin.

King David recognized the blessing of a heavenly Guide to help him navigate the challenges of life. "Show me your ways, LORD," he prayed, "teach me your paths. Guide me in your truth and teach me, for you are God my Savior, and my hope is in you all day long" (Psalm 25:4–5).

David may have taught his son Solomon to do this as well. As the wisest man on earth, Solomon knew where to find the ultimate source of wisdom. "Trust in the LORD with all your heart," he wrote in Proverbs 3:5–6, "and lean not on your own understanding; in all your ways submit to him, and he will make your paths straight."

As my husband did, God will guide us around the potholes of life—but we must follow Him. David's lead wouldn't have done me any good if I'd barreled along, bent on going my own way. I had to keep my eyes on him and follow his lead. And learn from his example.

So it is with God. He offers us His guidance through His Word, His Spirit, and His church, but He won't force us to follow Him.

Walking in His ways won't guarantee we'll never lose a hubcap. The occasional life pothole happens to even the most devoted. Following His lead will, however, help us avoid many of them.

After enduring the shame of my sin and suffering the pain of my losses, count me in.

Embrace the Truth: Lord, I believe You'll guide me around the potholes of life and down the path of righteousness.

Declare Your Faith: Show me Your ways, Lord. Teach me Your paths. Guide me in Your truth and teach me, for You are God my Savior, and my hope is in You all day long.

I believe . . .

The Holy Spirit abides with me forever

I will pray the Father, and He will give you another Helper, that He may abide with you forever—the Spirit of truth.

John 14:16–17 NKJV

When my daughter and son-in-law drove across the country to their new home in Washington state, Halsey, their French bulldog, was confused. Every night for more than a week, his owners parked at a different hotel, hauled their suitcases into a different hotel room, and unpacked what he needed for the night's stay—his food and water bowls, his bed, and enough kibble for dinner and breakfast. As soon as the sun rose, they packed up their stuff and drove to a different state.

Then one day everything changed. Instead of unpacking the essentials at a hotel, his owners carried all his stuff into an apartment. They set up his crate in their bedroom, his bed in the living room, and his food bowls in the kitchen. Wonder of wonder, his toy basket appeared—filled with all his favorite things—at the end of the hallway. They hung his leash on a hook near the front door and stowed his treats in the cupboard.

That's when Halsey realized he was home. No more driving. No more coming and going. No more goodbyes. He was there to stay.

Old Testament believers experienced a coming and going of a different sort than Halsey's. They experienced the coming and going of the Holy Spirit.

Before Christ's ascension, the Holy Spirit, the third member of the Trinity, came and went from believers. He'd fill and equip them for a season of ministry, and when they'd completed the task or season, He'd leave. He lived *with* them, not *in* them.

But when Christ returned to His Father, He ushered in a new era—a Spirit-led, Spirit-infused era. "I will not leave you as orphans," He promised His disciples (John 14:18). "[The Father] will give you another Helper, that He may abide with you forever" (v. 16 NKJV).

This beautiful word, *abide,* is the Greek word *meno*. Here it has the meaning of remaining as a constant, ever-dependable presence. At the moment of salvation, God sends the Holy Spirit to abide within us forever. He doesn't just show up and leave. He moves in (Ephesians 1:13–14). He saves (Romans 8:10–11), sanctifies (2 Thessalonians 2:13), teaches (John 14:26), comforts (Romans 15:13), intercedes (Romans 8:26), convicts (John 16:8), and empowers (Acts 1:8).

Jobs and circumstances may require Halsey and his family to move again, but God makes His home in us forever.

What a comfort. What a joy!

Embrace the Truth: God, in the person of the Holy Spirit makes His home in us—forever.

Declare Your Faith: Lord, I believe You have placed Your Spirit inside me to live with me forever. Jesus said so, and I believe Him. Thank You for the precious gift of Your forever presence. I never need to fear being separated from Your love, guidance, power, or presence. Thank You for being not only with me but in me.

I believe . . .

I can be great in God's kingdom

Whoever wants to become great among
you must be your servant.
Matthew 20:26

"We need to put down our phones, get up off our couch, and go serve somebody."

Our pastor wasn't mincing words one Sunday morning. As the text of his message flashed upon the screen, we saw why. "Jesus knew that the hour had come for him to leave this world and go to the Father. Having loved his own who were in the world, he loved them to the end. . . . So he got up from the meal . . . and began to wash his disciples' feet" (John 13:1, 4–5).

"On the night before Jesus was crucified," our pastor said, "He didn't take a vacation or treat Himself to a fancy dinner. He got up and served those He loved. He did the job no one wanted to do—wash the disciples' nasty feet."

He let his words sink in. "Jesus didn't just say He loved His disciples; He showed it by serving them. Love isn't words," he concluded. "Love is action."

I wonder if the apostle James was reflecting on that night in the upper room when he wrote, "Be doers of the word, and not hearers only, deceiving yourselves" (James 1:22 NKJV). The New International Version says it this way: "Do not merely listen to the word, and so deceive yourselves. Do what it says."

I'm embarrassed to admit this, but sometimes, I'd much rather be a hearer than a doer. I love listening to sermons, podcasts, and Christian music. I enjoy digging into Bible passages and uncovering treasure. I delight in talking about God's Word with other Christians.

But when I encounter a passage that sounds more like work than wonder, I'm tempted to write it on my To Do Later list instead of on my To Do Now list.

I talk about how Jesus loves me so much that He died for me, but I have to pray about helping in the church nursery or restocking the food pantry. Really?

Someone once described Christians as "Jesus with skin on," but this is only true if the skin is connected to hands and feet. To a body that demonstrates God's love through Spirit-directed actions. We look most like Jesus when we serve others.

Jesus, who is God with skin on, "knew that the Father had put all things under his power, and that he had come from God and was returning to God; so he got up . . . and began to wash his disciples' feet" (John 13:3–5).

His example compels me to ask, "What would God have me, an image bearer of God and recipient of His love, do to serve those around me?" I'll never know unless I'm willing to get up in obedience and kneel down in service.

I really want to be like Jesus. I suspect you would too. Thankfully, we don't have to wonder how to make it happen. Jesus told His disciples:

"Whoever wants to become great among you must be your servant . . . just as the Son of Man did not come to be served, but to serve, and to give his life as a ransom for many" (Matthew 20:26, 28).

Let's put down our phones, get up off our couch, and go serve somebody.

Embrace the Truth: We'll never accomplish true greatness until we get up in obedience and kneel down in service.

Declare Your Faith: Lord, I believe I can be great in Your kingdom, and that the pathway to greatness is through serving You by serving others. It seems counterintuitive, but so much of the faith life doesn't play by the world's rules. Maybe this is why You call us to walk by faith, not by sight. Help me, kind Father, trust You enough to get up in obedience and serve in humility—in Jesus's name.

I believe . . .

I have a choice

I will rejoice in the Lord, I will be joyful in God my Savior.
Habakkuk 3:18

"How have you survived?"

Six months had passed since my friend Marie's husband, Bill, died in a tragic car accident. David and I had attended the out-of-state funeral, but this was our first chance to talk face-to-face. Chocolate croissants, fresh from the oven, sat untouched between us. We cradled steaming mugs of Wild Orange tea, more for comfort than for warmth, as I asked Marie the hard questions deep friendships allow.

"Your entire world changed in an instant," I said. "Forty years of marriage, the ministry you shared, the plans you had for retirement . . ." I shook my head, aching at the breadth of her loss.

She nodded and gazed out the window, remembering. "The first week, I was numb. But one morning, I was in that fuzzy place between awake and asleep. I stretched out my arm as I always do, to reach for Bill, and he wasn't there." She swallowed and spoke again.

"Everything came rushing back. The accident, the hospital, the funeral.

"I realized, in the first moment of clarity I'd experienced since I got that horrible call, I had a choice to make. I could turn toward God or away from Him."

She raised her eyes to meet mine. Tears shimmered but didn't fall. "I chose to turn toward Him. God's presence every day is the only way I've survived."

She took a deep breath, then lifted the mug to her lips. Two sips, and then she continued.

"I'd been studying the book of Habakkuk, of all things, and I remembered his declaration at the end. Our Bible study leader made us memorize it." She searched her memory and then quoted verses 17 and 18 of the third chapter: "'Though the fig tree does not bud and there are no grapes on the vines, though the olive crop fails and the fields produce no food, though there are no sheep in the pen and no cattle in the stalls, yet I will rejoice in the LORD, I will be joyful in God my Savior.'

"I decided to trust God. He's my only hope."

Not everyone who experiences a tragedy like Marie's turns toward God. Some forsake the faith—and the God—they claim to follow.

This falling away isn't a modern phenomenon. The disciples in Jesus's day struggled too.

Unlike many of today's preachers, who promise Christians a life of ease, prosperity, and happiness, Jesus often spoke of the cost of true discipleship. One such conversation caused many of His disciples to turn away.

Looking at the Twelve, He asked, "You do not want to leave too, do you?" (John 6:67).

Simon Peter spoke for them all. "Lord, to whom shall we go? You have the words of eternal life" (v. 68).

Peter knew the world offered no hope. Only Jesus could make sense of tragedies, carry him through trials, and one day make everything right again.

Marie knows too. This is why, every morning, she opens her Bible, bows her head, and prays. "God, I have no idea what today holds, but I choose to walk with You. You are my Savior and my joy."

Habakkuk, Peter, and Marie remind us that every day, no matter what happens, we have a choice.

Will we trust God with our hurts and hardships? Believe He has a good purpose, even when His purposes cause pain? Will we seek our joy in Him instead of in our circumstances?

What choice will you make?

Embrace the Truth: No matter what we face, we can choose to trust God our Savior.

Declare Your Faith: Lord, I believe that in every situation I can trust You. When I do, I experience joy that transcends my suffering and eclipses my trials. Help me, when hardship and loss weaken my faith, to always turn toward You. Amen.

I believe . . .

Jesus is coming back

If I go and prepare a place for you, I will come back and take you to be with me that you also may be where I am.

John 14:3

Mom hugged me—a little too hard and a little too long—as we stood in the doorway one frosty February morning. "I won't be here when you get home from school."

I looked at her, puzzled. Mom was always home when my sisters and I came home from school.

She smoothed the bangs from my eyes and tucked a wayward strand of hair under my crocheted cap.

"Why not?"

"I have to have an operation," she said, choosing her words carefully. "I have to stay in the hospital for about a week."

My mouth flew open as she spoke faster. "Don't worry. Granny's going to come stay with you, and Dad will be home at night. I need you to be brave."

I nodded, struggling to make sense of the words.

"Everything's going to be fine," she said. "Now, scoot. You're gonna be late for school."

As I walked to school, my mind whirled. I was ten—old enough to know that not everyone who goes into the hospital comes out again.

I made it two blocks before fear overwhelmed me and I burst into tears. I turned toward home, running as fast as my galoshes-clad feet would take me. Mom must have heard me clumping up the porch steps, because before I reached the door, she'd opened it. I fell into her arms and cried out all the tears that hadn't frozen on my cheeks.

"I love you, Mom," I said, squeezing her hard. "I don't want you to go."

"I love you too," she said, "and I don't want to go. But I have to."

She wiped my tears with her thumbs, swiped at her own eyes, then planted a kiss on my forehead. She pointed me to the door with a gentle shove.

"I'll be home soon. I promise."

The Gospels tell a story of another emotional parting. As the time for Jesus's departure neared, He didn't want His disciples to be caught by surprise. He shared increasingly graphic details about His upcoming death and resurrection (Matthew 16:21). On the night before He was crucified, He told them clearly. "You heard me say, 'I am going away and I am coming back to you.' . . . I have told you now before it happens, so that when it does happen you will believe" (John 14:28–29).

Jesus knew His foreknowledge of His death and resurrection would show His disciples that His arrest, trial, and crucifixion wasn't a heinous crime against an innocent man. It was the sovereign plan of God to bring about humanity's redemption.

Jesus wasn't a victim. He was the victor.

When I returned from school that sad February day, Mom wasn't there. But a week later, she came back—just as she promised.

When the disciples huddled in an upper room thousands of years ago, Jesus wasn't there. But three days later, He came back—not from a hospital, but from the dead. Just as He promised.

Someday soon, He'll return again—this time to take us home to be with Him forever.

How do I know?

He promised.

Embrace the Truth: Jesus *is* coming back.

Declare Your Faith: Lord, I believe You will return one day to take us home to be with You forever. Forgive me when I grow weary (and sometimes doubt) as I wait for the blessed hope and glorious appearing of our great God and Savior Jesus Christ (Titus 2:13). You've kept every other promise You made. I have no reason to doubt You now. Even so, come, Lord Jesus!

I believe . . .

Jesus is God

About the Son [God] says, "Your throne, O God,
will last for ever and ever; a scepter of justice
will be the scepter of your kingdom."
Hebrews 1:8

I listened closely as my mentor talked with the man sitting beside us in a coffee shop.

In a divinely appointed moment, Chad had started the spiritual conversation. He'd seen our Bibles open before us. When we bowed our heads over our scones, he took note. Although his eyes remained focused on the book in front of him, the subtle expressions that flickered across his face—a furrowed forehead, a raised eyebrow—showed me he was listening to our conversation.

Finally, he raised his eyes. "Excuse me," he said. "Are you Christians?"

"Yes, we are," my mentor replied. "Are you?"

"Well," he said, "I think Jesus was a good man. And a good teacher."

"Then you must believe Jesus is God," my mentor said. "After all, He claimed to be God (John 8:58; 10:30, 33). Good men and good teachers don't lie."

Besides Jesus's testimony, the first chapter of Hebrews contains several compelling reasons to believe in Jesus's deity. Most significant is that God the Father declared Jesus is God.

God is Jesus's most credible reference.

"About the Son [God] says, 'Your throne, O God, will last for ever and ever; a scepter of justice will be the scepter of your kingdom'" (Hebrews 1:8). God the Father called Jesus *God.*

As an appropriate acknowledgment to Jesus's deity, He commanded, "Let all God's angels worship him" (Hebrews 1:6). God the Father wasn't seeking to honor Jesus as a good man or even a good prophet or teacher by sharing His worship with Him. Oh, no. "I will not yield my glory to another or my praise to idols," He said in Isaiah 42:8. When He commanded the angels to worship Jesus, God the Father declared Jesus was worthy of worship—because He is God.

Remember the first command God gave Moses on Mt. Sinai? "I am the LORD your God. . . . You shall have no other gods before me" (Exodus 20:2–3). If Jesus wasn't God, God the Father wouldn't have told the angels to break this command by telling them to worship another—unless that "other" was God.

The writer of Hebrews describes it this way, "The Son is the radiance of God's glory and the exact representation of his being" (1:3). Similarly, Jesus told Philip, "Anyone who has seen me has seen the Father" (John 14:9).

One day, hallelujah, we'll see Jesus face-to-face. We'll worship our Savior and creator in the Trinity's unity—God the Father, Son, and Spirit.

Until then, we can worship Him as my mentor did—by faithfully pointing people like the man in the coffee shop to Him.

Embrace the Truth: I believe Jesus is God.

Declare Your Faith: God, I don't pretend to understand the Trinity, how one God can exist in three persons, but I don't have to. I can rest in what Your Word says—that Jesus is God. Thank You for allowing me to get to know You through the person of Jesus Christ. I'm so grateful He took on human form, lived a sinless life, and offered His life as payment for my sin. I can't wait to sing with the angels, "All hail the pow'r of Jesus's name! Let angels prostrate fall. Bring forth the royal diadem, and crown Him Lord of all!"[5]

I believe . . .
God can restore

I will restore to you the years that the
swarming locust has eaten.
Joel 2:25 ESV

David and I hadn't seen Jeremy in years, but there he was, seated two pews ahead of us in the sanctuary. And he wasn't alone. On his left sat his wife, Sandy. To his right sat his children, Mya and Ben.

As I watched, he draped his arm across the back of the pew, patted Sandy's shoulder, and gave a gentle squeeze. Mya scooted closer and leaned her head against his shoulder. Their tender gestures made tears spring to my eyes.

After the service, we found Jeremy balancing a cup of punch and a slice of cake. When David called his name, he looked up and grinned.

"Man, I am so glad to see you," Jeremy said.

"Not half as glad as I am to see you," David replied. Jeremy set his food aside and wrapped an arm around David's shoulders. They drifted off to a quiet corner. Soon they were deep in conversation.

Years before, a series of indiscretions had brought Jeremy and Sandy weeks away from a divorce. Jeremy was unrepentant, and Sandy was heartbroken. Our pastor counseled, and our congregation prayed, but nothing seemed to change.

Until the day he returned to church. At the end of the service, he came forward and wept in our pastor's arms.

Jeremy's job transferred them away almost immediately after, but in the intervening years, God worked a miracle in their family.

Their story is a modern illustration of God's promise to Judah during the nation's years of rebellion.

> "Yet even now," declares the LORD,
> "return to me with all your heart,
> with fasting, with weeping, and with mourning;
> and rend your hearts and not your garments."
> Return to the LORD your God,
> for he is gracious and merciful,
> slow to anger, and abounding in steadfast love.
> (Joel 2:12–13 ESV)

Jeremy found forgiveness when he came to God in genuine repentance. Sadly, Israel did not. They stubbornly remained in their sin through locust plagues, fire, and famine. Finally God sent the Babylonian army to conquer and destroy their nation.

His promise, however, still stands. Scripture tells us that during the day of the Lord, Judah will return to God (Jeremiah 30:3).

As Jeremy did, they'll experience the promise of Joel 2:25: "I will restore to you the years that the swarming locust has eaten."

"It's taken us a long time to work through the hurt and pain I caused my family," Jeremy told David. "I had to earn back their trust and rebuild our lives. But God has been gracious. He's restored our family. In some ways, we're stronger than we've ever been before" (ESV).

Not every story has a happy ending like Jeremy's, at least on this earth. Actions have consequences. But we can rest in the promise that if we repent and turn to God, He'll welcome us home and begin His work of restoration. And if we're the ones others have sinned against? His restoration power can free us from bitterness and heal our heart. We can trust Him.

Embrace the Truth: God can restore even the most unrestorable life in ways we never dreamed possible.

Declare Your Faith: Lord, I believe You can restore what seems hopelessly broken in my life. I've seen You do it—in marriages, families, health, relationships, finances. Nothing is too hard for You. Thank You for the promise of Joel 3 that strengthens my fainting heart and encourages my faith. You know the broken person or situation that weighs most heavily on my heart right now. I give ____________________ to You and ask You to restore that person or those circumstances. Help me continue to pray and not lose heart. In the strong name of Jesus I ask. Amen.

I believe . . .

God is trustworthy

The eternal God is your refuge, and
underneath are the everlasting arms.

Deuteronomy 33:27

"If she doesn't learn to trust me," the swim instructor said, "she'll never learn to swim. She has to move outside her comfort zone, or she'll always play it safe."

My young daughter had eagerly embraced swim lessons. She loved splashing in the shallows, blowing bubbles in the water, and even dunking her face. But when her instructor asked her to step off the diving board? Uh-uh. No way.

It didn't matter that her instructor walked to the end of the board with her. Or that another instructor waited in the water to catch her. It was scary, and she wasn't doing it. How such a tiny girl could put up such a big fight, I don't know, but fight she did. She argued. She bargained. She cried. She looked at me to rescue her, but I refused to make eye contact.

Finally, the instructor took her by the arms and gently lowered her off the diving board. Almost before her toes touched the water, the other instructor caught her and eased her into the pool. "Now, swim to the side," she said, and gave her a nudge.

My daughter paddled to the edge, climbed out, and strode over to me. "Did you see me, Mom?" she said. "I went off the diving board!"

Some days, I feel as though I'm standing at the edge of a diving board looking into the water and saying, "Uh-uh, no way." No way I'm going to talk with that person about her faith. No way I'm going to step into the depths of a relational challenge. No way I'm going to stand up for what I believe when everyone around me disagrees.

Then God says, "Trust Me." Jesus says, "I'll catch you." And the Holy Spirit says, "I won't leave you."

On good days, I step out in faith. I take a risk and find God faithful. Even if I get my face wet or struggle a bit, I grow in confidence and strength. This makes me more willing to jump in the next time I sense His gentle (or not-so-gentle) nudge.

Sometimes I go under, but I feel His arms supporting me (Deuteronomy 33:27). "Good try," I sense Him saying. "What will you do differently next time?"

Even in my failure I succeed, because success in the Christian life is about obedience, not results.

My reluctant swimmer-girl went on to swim competitively. She became a lifeguard and a swim instructor. I've never had the opportunity to watch her teach, but I can imagine her telling her students what God often tells me: "Trust me. Jump in. I won't leave you."

Embrace the Truth: When I take a leap of faith, God will catch me.

Declare Your Faith: Lord, I believe You'll accomplish Your good purposes each time I step out in faith. Lead me to do Your will, even when I'm afraid. Give me courage to obey, even when it's hard. Catch me when I mess up, and help me feel Your pleasure even when I don't see results. In Jesus's name I pray, amen.

I believe . . .

I should pray

Pray without ceasing.
1 Thessalonians 5:17 ESV

I'll be honest. Sometimes I grow discouraged in my prayers.

I pray for good things and don't always see the results I hope for. Troubled marriages continue to disintegrate. Sick people grow sicker. Lost loved ones seem to move farther from God instead of drawing near. During my lowest times I wonder, Why bother?

Thankfully, God's Word talks me off the ledge of prayerlessness and inspires me to press on. If you're wondering if prayer is all that important, Jesus's example, His teaching, and the witness of believers settles it.

Scripture records twenty-five examples of Jesus praying. Luke 5:16 reveals that "Jesus often withdrew to lonely places and prayed." He sought God's guidance before making important decisions (6:12–13). He met with God in prayer before and after a long day of ministry (Mark 1:35; 6:46). At Lazarus's tomb, he thanked God for hearing His prayer and raising His friend from the dead (John 11:41–42).

During Jesus's time on earth, He set aside the voluntary use of His deity to become like us. He sought God, as we do, for guidance, wisdom, and power. His consistent example affirms that believers should pray.

Jesus also expected His followers to pray. "One day Jesus was praying in a certain place. When he finished, one of his disciples said to him, 'Lord, teach us to pray, just as John taught his disciples.' He said to them, 'When you pray, say: "Father . . ."'" (Luke 11:1–2).

His disciples knew Jesus's prayers were powerful and effective. They watched Him talk to God and saw God answer. They wanted wisdom, courage, and power like Jesus had and suspected prayer was the key. Jesus knew it was, which is why He introduced His teaching by saying, "*When* you pray," not "*If* you pray." Prayer wasn't optional. It was imperative.

History records how devout believers down through the ages have sought God through prayer. The apostle Paul wrote about prayer more than forty times.

John Wesley prayed with an open Bible, knowing God would speak to him through His Word.[6] George Mueller, best known for running orphanages in England that cared for more than ten thousand children, committed to pray for five lost individuals. In his lifetime, three came to know the Lord. The remaining two surrendered their lives to Christ after Mueller's death. Mueller had prayed for them for more than fifty-two years.[7] Spiritual giants like Martin Luther, D. L. Moody, and Billy Graham spent hours on their knees before the Lord.

Jesus's example, His teaching, and the witness of countless believers affirm the command of 1 Thessalonians that we should "pray without ceasing" (5:17 ESV). These and a multitude of other reasons strengthen our spiritual backbone when we grow weary in prayer.

Embrace the Truth: When we wonder if prayer is important, Jesus's example, His teaching, and the witness of believers down through the ages encourage us to press on.

Declare Your Faith: Lord, I believe You call us to pray because You work in mighty ways through prayer. When I grow weary or doubtful, remind me of this. Make me a mighty prayer warrior for You!

I believe . . .

I've received Christ's righteousness

God made him who had no sin to be sin for us, so that in him we might become the righteousness of God.

2 Corinthians 5:21

"Never enough."

When I asked my friend, Laura, how she was feeling, I didn't expect this answer. I knew she'd been busy at work and struggling to balance family and church responsibilities, but her reply hinted at something more than work/life balance.

"Ever since I was a little girl, I've always felt like I was never enough. Dad was hard on us. If I gave eighty percent, he'd ask for eighty-five. If I gave eighty-five, he'd ask for ninety. I swear, if I somehow gave one hundred percent, he'd ask for a hundred and ten." Her voice rose, then dropped. "I always felt like I disappointed him."

"The sad thing is," she said, taking a deep breath, "I feel the same way about God. I try to please Him, to live a moral life, read my Bible every day, and serve at church, but I never feel like I'm good enough." She sighed.

"And I'm not even talking about real sin issues, like the way I yell at my husband and my kids." Resting her elbows on the table, she cupped her face in her hands and frowned. "Deep down inside, I wonder if He's always disappointed in me—like my father was."

"What would you say if I told you that when God looks at you, He sees the righteousness of Christ?"

"Ha," Laura said. "I wish."

"I'm serious." I grabbed my phone, scrolled to 2 Corinthians 5, and held it out. "Read verse 21."

She squinted at the screen. "God made him who had no sin to be sin for us, so that in him we might become the righteousness of God."

"See?" I said. "Jesus did the hard work. He took every sin we'll ever commit and traded it for His righteousness on the cross. He took our 'never enough' and gave us His 'more than enough.' This is how God sees us." I slowed my speech to emphasize every word. "We don't have to work to satisfy Him. If we've trusted in Christ to save us, Jesus satisfied Him for us."

I looked deep into Laura's eyes and saw a hopeful glint.

"But everybody knows we're supposed to live a certain way and do good things," she said. "Where does that fit in?"

"Our good works are our thank you—because we love Him, not because we're trying to meet some impossible standard."

Her shoulders lifted—just a smidge.

"You're not 'enough,'" I said, "and neither am I. But Jesus is."

For the first time that morning, Laura smiled.

Embrace the Truth: When Jesus died on the cross, He took our sinfulness and gave us His righteousness.

Declare Your Faith: Lord, I believe You became sin for me so I might receive Your holy, perfect righteousness. Thank You. Help me live out the righteousness You've placed within me because of gratitude and love for You. I want to honor You in all I do. In Jesus's precious name I pray, amen.

I believe . . .

God calls me to practice hospitality

Offer hospitality to one another without grumbling.
1 Peter 4:9

As seventeen-year-old David came forward at the end of the church service to surrender his life to Christ, one couple, Charlie and Rhonda Smoak, looked on with interest. David's long hair touched his shoulders, and his eyes still held a hint of the alcohol he'd consumed the night before. But he seemed sincere. Desperate to change his ways, he knew he needed Someone more powerful than himself to take control of his life.

"God, help me," he prayed. And God did.

David became an eager and active member of the church. He attended youth group and read his Bible. Hungry to learn, he asked lots of questions. And Charlie, a young husband with two small boys, saw David's potential.

"Would you like to meet once a week to study the Bible?" he asked after Sunday service. "You can come for dinner, and afterward we'll talk about what we've read."

David jumped at the chance. He wanted to study the Bible. He also wanted to visit Charlie and Rhonda's home. His parents had divorced years before, and sitting around the table with a couple who loved each other and loved God sounded appealing.

Every Tuesday night for more than a year, David joined Charlie and Rhonda for a simple dinner and Bible study. Under Charlie's careful tutelage, he memorized verses, learned the major events of the New Testament, and grew in his faith.

He also experienced the joy of Christian hospitality. He watched how Charlie and Rhonda honored and respected each other—even when they disagreed. He saw how they disciplined their boys in love instead of anger, and he listened as they prayed. Over tacos and tea, fried chicken and Chinese takeout, Charlie and Rhonda modeled the Christian life to David.

The apostle Peter, pastoring the church in Jerusalem, encouraged believers to "offer hospitality to one another without grumbling" (1 Peter 4:9). Paul did too, encouraging Roman believers to "share with the Lord's people who are in need. Practice hospitality" (Romans 12:13).

In many circles, hospitality is rare. We're busier than ever, and hospitality costs time, money, and effort. But oh, the rewards that await those who practice it.

Gathering together—whether over a five-course feast or a frozen pizza—knits our hearts together and strengthens our faith. It extends our Christian influence and satisfies physical and emotional needs. When we extend hospitality to strangers, we may even entertain angels unaware (Hebrews 13:2).

With Charlie and Rhonda's help, God took that long-haired boy with an alcohol problem from a broken home and made him into a godly husband—my husband. He's also a godly father and minster of the gospel who loves to extend hospitality in Jesus's name.

I don't know where my husband would be if the Smoaks hadn't obeyed the Holy Spirit's nudge and opened their home and hearts to him. I'm thankful they did. Seeing David's life transformed and knowing they had a part is rewarding, but one day, Charlie and Rhonda will receive an even greater reward. "Then the King will say to those on his right, 'Come, you who are blessed by my Father; take your inheritance, the kingdom prepared for you since the creation of the world'" (Matthew 25:34).

"Truly I tell you, whatever you did for one of the least of these brothers and sisters of mine, you did for me" (v. 40).

Embrace the Truth: God calls Christians to practice biblical hospitality toward others.

Declare Your Faith: Lord, I believe You call me to extend hospitality in Your name. Open my eyes to those who, like David, need Christian fellowship. Help me look beyond the people I feel most comfortable with and reach out to the one who needs a meal, a listening ear, or a warm hug. Show me unsaved people too, who need to experience Christian love. Remind me that hospitality doesn't have to be hard. Sometimes it's as simple as giving a cup of cold water in Jesus's name.

I believe . . .

God calls me to praise Him

Let everything that has breath praise the Lord.
Psalm 150:6

Have you ever wondered why God commands us to praise Him?

Is He an egomaniac? A narcissist? Self-centered, vain, or insecure?

If you feel a little squirmy asking these questions, take comfort. I do too. To think such things about God, let alone ask, seems sacrilegious. We expect a divine stun gun to crackle from the sky at any moment.

Yet haven't you wondered, just once, why God commands every living thing on earth to praise Him? "Let everything that has breath praise the Lord," wrote the psalmist (Psalm 150:6). But why?

We've all been around people starving for praise. "Do you think I'm pretty?" "Do I look good in this outfit?" "Didn't I do well?"

We instinctively know those who seek praise feel insecure and need affirmation. But God isn't insecure or needy. He's the most majestic being in the universe. The creator of everything. All-knowing, all-seeing, all powerful.

So if He's not insecure, is He an egomaniac? It's not far fetched to suspect Someone this big must have an ego to match.

Except God is perfect and sinless. Pride can't exist within His holy heart.

So if He doesn't need us to tell Him how wise and wonderful He is, why command us to praise Him?

When I was six years old, I came face-to-face with a playground bully. This hulking second grader stared me down and declared, "If you don't give me your ice cream money, I'll punch you."

I didn't stand a chance.

But right before I handed over my quarter, I remembered someone bigger than me. Someone faster, smarter, and stronger. Someone who loved me.

"If you do," I said, squaring my puny shoulders and looking the bully in the eye, "my father will squash you like a bug. He's big. And strong. And eats bullies for lunch." I pointed to the knot of parents gathered at the edge of the playground and waved.

The bully's bravado whooshed out of his puffed-up chest like air escaping a balloon. A flicker of uncertainty shone in his arrogant eyes. He lowered his fists and wiped his clammy hands on his pants. Looking in the direction I pointed, he stuttered, "Oh, yeah, well, I'm gonna let you off this time, but I'll be watching you." He slunk off, and I breathed a sigh of relief.

Funny thing, my father wasn't in that knot of parents that day. He didn't need to be. He existed, and my act of declaring his might and power was enough to banish the bully who threatened me. Knowing Dad was my defender wiped the fear from my heart and helped me face the threat with confidence.

The same is true in our relationship with God. When we face the bullies of cancer, unemployment, wayward children's unbelief, or a struggling marriage, we need to remember we have an ally who's stronger than whatever threatens us.

This is one reason God commands us to praise Him. Every time we declare His power, wisdom, compassion, love, and faithfulness, we remind ourselves how big God is. We declare that He, not the bully, wins every time.

Does God need to be reminded how wonderful He is? No.

But we do.

Let everything that has breath praise the Lord.

Embrace the Truth: When I praise God, I remind myself that God is greater than anything I face.

Declare Your Faith: Lord, I believe I should praise You—not for Your good but for mine. My praise adds nothing to who You are. You're complete. Instead, my praise adds to my personal peace and strength. It multiplies my hope and joy. So often, when I grow fearful or overwhelmed, I forget who You are and the power of praise. Remind me, Lord, to praise You—in good times and bad, for You are worthy. Use my praise to strengthen my faith and the faith of those around me. In the mighty name of Jesus I pray, amen.

I believe . . .

God can transform my ending

Forgetting what is behind and straining toward what is ahead, I press on toward the goal to win the prize for which God has called me heavenward in Christ Jesus.

Philippians 3:13–14

"I'm sixty-five years old," Chris said to our pastor. "I've made more mistakes than Noah had animals on the ark. I've lied, cheated, and wronged a lot of people. I've been divorced twice, and my kids barely tolerate me. I believe God saved me, but I doubt He can do much with the life I have left."

"I look back on the years when my kids were little," Sarah said during a recent Bible study. "I was so focused on having a big house, a fulfilling career, and a perfect body that I neglected my kids. I saw them as inconveniences. Now that they're teenagers, I wish I had those years back. None of them are interested in spiritual things. I'm afraid I'm at least partially to blame."

Melissa was there for her kids, and she tried to raise them in the faith, but she often let anger control her. "I yelled a lot. I didn't realize how much my anger hurt them and our relationship. I've confessed my sin to God, but I doubt I can ever undo the damage."

Those who came to faith later in life often feel hopeless about their past sins. So do many who look back regretfully on certain periods in their life. Thankfully, God specializes in taking the broken pieces of our lives and rebuilding them.

The apostle Paul certainly had much to regret. In Acts 22:4, he told his listeners, "I persecuted the followers of this Way [Christians] to their death, arresting both men and women and throwing them into prison." Describing his heinous acts, he wrote, "I was once a blasphemer and a persecutor and a violent man" (1 Timothy 1:13).

After he placed his faith in Jesus, the consequences of Paul's past haunted him. Fellow Christians, terrified by his previous actions, avoided him. His reputation as an angry, vengeful man hindered him as he struggled to live out the new life he had in Christ.

Paul could have easily grown discouraged. Self-recrimination and the whispering voice of his accuser, Satan, could have derailed any good work God intended to do through him. Instead, he trusted God with the past and cooperated with Him to write a new future.

"Forgetting what is behind and straining toward what is ahead," he wrote, "I press on toward the goal to win the prize for which God has called me heavenward in Christ Jesus" (Philippians 3:13–14). Paul couldn't go back and change the beginning, but with God's help, he could change the ending.

We can do the same.

Chris did. As God brought people to mind that he had wronged, he reached out, apologized, and when possible, made restitution. He shared with them how God had changed his heart. Some, especially his adult children, were skeptical, but as he continued to walk out his new faith, they marveled at his transformation.

Sarah began by expressing her regrets to her teenagers and asking their forgiveness. She eliminated several activities from her schedule so she could be home more. Little by little, she's getting to know them again.

Melissa took each of her children out for breakfast individually. As they chowed down on waffles and bacon, she admitted her sin of anger and apologized for the hurt she'd caused. "I want to change. I've asked a friend to hold me accountable," she told them. "With God's help, I won't be an angry mom anymore."

Paul's transformation from a cold-blooded murderer to a big-hearted apostle gives hope to everyone with past regrets. Years later, he wrote that the same Christians who'd once avoided him now "praised God because of me" (Galatians 1:24).

With God's help, people will say the same about us.

Embrace the Truth: With God's help, I can overcome my past and embrace a new future.

Declare Your Faith: Lord, I believe You can transform my ending. I've hurt people, behaved in ways that don't honor You, and misspent opportunities You've given me. Help me, wherever I can, to make amends. Grant me a humble spirit to ask forgiveness. I know I must bear the consequences of my actions, but I also know You have the power to restore the years the locusts have eaten. In Your mercy, heal and restore. Transform me so dramatically that everyone who sees me will glorify You. In the strong name of Jesus I ask, amen.

I believe . . .

God wants me to be part of a church

. . . not giving up meeting together, as some are in the habit of doing, but encouraging one another—and all the more as you see the Day approaching.

Hebrews 10:25

"We were missing out on one of the sweetest parts of the Christian life, and we didn't even realize it."

Debbie, a lovely woman with dark hair and puppy-dog eyes, was speaking to our church family one Sunday. "We thought it was enough to be 'spiritual,'" she said, punctuating "spiritual" with air quotes. "We can worship God anywhere, we told ourselves. Out in nature. Online. Reading our Bibles alone in the study."

She paused.

"Then I read Hebrews 10:25, '. . . not giving up meeting together, as some are in the habit of doing.' I realized God loved the church. Jesus gave His life for it, and He wants us to be a part of it. We need them, and they need us.

"We've been here ever since." She looked around at her brothers and sisters in Christ and smiled. "And we're very glad. Fellowshipping with other believers, learning God's Word together, and serving God with you has made our lives so much richer."

Debbie and her husband realized what so many today miss—that Christianity apart from the church is an anemic substitute for what God designed.

The book of Acts describes how, when people placed their

faith in Christ, God added them to the church (Acts 2:47). Not only to the universal church, the worldwide family of believers, but to the local church—the church in Jerusalem, where they met together daily.

Paul's letter to the church at Colossae describes God's plan: "Let the message of Christ dwell among you richly as you teach and admonish one another with all wisdom through psalms, hymns, and songs from the Spirit, singing to God with gratitude in your hearts" (Colossians 3:16). Gathering with fellow believers encourages us and builds us up in the faith.

God called the apostles and believers not only to evangelize but to disciple. Discipleship happens best through a local body of believers. If we could do this on our own, why would Paul, after leading people to the Lord, appoint pastors, elders, and deacons to minister through local churches?

Just as God places physical babies into physical families, He places spiritual babies into spiritual families. The family of God, the local church, is God's plan to help Christians of all ages and stages grow, learn, mature, serve, and fulfill the Great Commission.

God knows the flaws and frailties of His body, the church, yet He calls us to be a part of it. "Christ loved the church and gave himself up for her to make her holy, cleansing her by the washing with water through the word, and to present her to himself as a radiant church, without stain or wrinkle or any other blemish, but holy and blameless" (Ephesians 5:25–27).

As my friend Debbie discovered, Christ loves the church, and we should too.

Embrace the Truth: God knows the flaws and frailties of His body, the church, yet He calls us to be a part of it.

Declare Your Faith: Lord, I believe it's Your will that I be a faithful, committed part of Your church. If You loved it enough to die to bring it into existence, then it must be pretty important. Thank

You for creating a family of believers I can do life with. Reveal to me any wrong thinking I might have about the church and show me Your will for my church attendance. Help me love the church as You love it. In Jesus's name I pray, amen.

I believe . . .

I'll find God

You will seek me and find me when you seek me with all your heart.

Jeremiah 29:13

For twenty-eight days, my friend Don sought a special treasure. Everywhere he went, he looked for dropped coins. He found them too. Pennies mostly, but now and then he spotted a nickel or a quarter.

"I make the most of every opportunity to find coins," Don said in one of his social media posts. "I scan the parking lot as I walk into a store, look on the ground by the cash registers, and jog through drive thrus when I go out for runs if they are on my route. Sometimes I make sure they're on my route. My goal is to find at least one every day."

Don's commitment to walk through his days with his eyes open for coins reminded me of a story my pastor told years ago. On the way to visit a church member who'd just been diagnosed with terminal cancer, he prayed for words to encourage her. By the time he arrived, he knew what the Lord wanted him to say.

"Every day," he challenged the woman, "look for evidences of God's presence. Keep your eyes open. You'll find them."

She did, and God revealed Himself to her in sweet and profound ways.

I wonder what we'd see if we approached each day looking for God. One morning I decided to walk through that day intentionally looking for Him. I began by looking in His Word, the most important place to look for Him. Through the prophet Jeremiah,

God promised: "You will seek me and find me when you seek me with all your heart" (Jeremiah 29:13).

In the breeze's coolness, I witnessed God's restorative and refreshing presence (31:25). In the pink dawn, I saw how His mercies are new every morning (Isaiah 50:4). In the kittens tumbling around on my neighbor's lawn, I glimpsed His humor and creativity (Psalm 104:24). I experienced His bountiful heart as I watched abundant rain fall on our thirsty neighborhood (Jeremiah 5:24). In a neighbor's wave, I spied His desire to bless His children with relationships (1 John 4:11).

Everywhere I turned, God was there.

Today, if you long to see that God is alive, active, and at work in the world, look around. As Don searched for coins, make the most of every opportunity to look for God. Scan the horizon. Look high and look low. You will see Him everywhere.

Don's coin hunting streak ended when he went to bed at 10:52 p.m. on day 28. He'd looked all that day but never found a coin.

Thankfully, we'll never have this problem with God. If we seek Him with all our hearts, we will find Him. Aren't you glad?

Embrace the Truth: When I search for God like a hidden treasure, I will find Him.

Declare Your Faith: Father, I believe I'll find You when I search for You with all my heart. Thank You for Your willingness to reveal Yourself to us. Forgive me for being lazy in my pursuit of You. You are my greatest treasure, but sometimes I lose sight of this. Make me eager to seek You.

I believe . . .

God never wastes suffering

Our light and momentary troubles are achieving for us an eternal glory that far outweighs them all.
2 Corinthians 4:17

Have you ever watched someone you love suffer? Or maybe you've been the one who suffered. You love God with all your heart, and you hoped your love for Him would shield you from the ravages of this broken world. But it hasn't.

You've experienced the crushing agony of a wayward child, a failed marriage, or a health crisis. You lost your ministry, your job, or your family. A friend betrayed you, or a parent failed you when you needed them the most. Wave after suffocating wave of grief threatens to drown you, and your heart—the heart that seeks to follow hard after God—faints. Why, Lord? Why me? Why them?

The apostle Paul treaded the stormy waters of trial. Listen to the words he chose to describe his life: "We are hard pressed . . . perplexed . . . persecuted . . . struck down" (2 Corinthians 4:8–9). Paul and his companions weren't having an oh-gosh-I-spilled-coffee-on-my-pants kind of bad day. They were "under great pressure, far beyond [their] ability to endure, so that [they] despaired of life itself" (1:8).

Why?

Why would God allow Paul to suffer beatings, shipwrecks (more than one), imprisonments, persecution, and a relentless, incurable "thorn in the flesh"? Wouldn't it make more sense to wrap him in impenetrable bubble roll and give him an armed guard to clear the way?

Amazingly, Paul didn't complain. Instead, he shared how God was using his suffering to further the kingdom. "Now I want you to know, brothers and sisters, that what has happened to me has actually served to advance the gospel" (Philippians 1:12). God's power, not Paul's, was being displayed (2 Corinthians 4:7).

Sometimes we and other Christians suffer in heinous ways. We ask God to ease our pain, change our circumstances, or free us from our trial. Instead, God uses the frailty of our circumstances and the mortality of our bodies to spotlight the forever, joy-filled immortality that awaits us.

"Though outwardly we are wasting away, yet inwardly we are being renewed day by day," Paul wrote. "For our light and momentary troubles are achieving for us *an eternal glory that far outweighs them all* (vv. 16–17 emphasis added). Paul knew—and we can know too—God never wastes suffering.

What do we do when we suffer and life overwhelms us?

"We fix our eyes not on what is seen, but on what is unseen, since what is seen is temporary, but what is unseen is eternal" (v. 18). We press in harder to God. We pray more, share what God is teaching us, and commit our souls to His good purposes.

And we believe God is accomplishing far more than we could ever imagine as we trust Him in our suffering.

Embrace the Truth: God uses our temporary suffering to produce an eternal weight of glory.

Declare Your Faith: Father, I believe You never waste suffering. I can't begin to understand how You can bring good out of the tragedies You allow into our lives, but I've seen You do it. The Bible testifies how You bring beauty from ashes, and I've experienced this in my life. Help me trust You when I don't understand. Use my suffering and the sufferings of others to accomplish Your good purposes in the world. In Jesus's name I ask, amen.

I believe . . .

I exist to glorify God

The life [Christ] lives, he lives to God.

Romans 6:10

Say *Brandenburg Concertos* and every classical music lover will respond, "Johann Sebastian Bach." And who hasn't attended a wedding where "Jesu, Joy of Man's Desiring," based on one of Bach's concertos, set the tone for the event?

Regarded as one of the greatest composers in the history of Western music, Bach created hundreds of sacred and secular works. His goal? "To dispel sadness and bring joy."[8]

Even if I studied music for decades, I'd never be a world-class musician. I can barely sing the notes of "Jesus Loves Me" to my grandchildren without making the dog howl. Nevertheless, Bach inspires me. If you search the internet or view a handwritten copy of one of Bach's musical scores, you'll see why.

At the top of the page, you might notice the initials JJ. At the bottom, SDG.

Before Bach composed a score or wrote a note, he often wrote JJ, an abbreviation for the Latin phrase *Jesu juva*, "Jesus help." He could have presumptuously dived in and relied on his training, experience, and giftedness to write his musical scores. Instead, Bach paused to ask Jesus to help.

When he finished, Bach penned the initialism SDG, Latin for *soli Deo gloria*—"for God's glory alone." These simple letters reminded him and everyone who would read his music that God, not Bach, deserved the glory, honor, and praise.

The apostle Paul similarly encouraged believers to live each day in God, through God, and for God. He daily fought the temptation to rely on his training under the esteemed teacher Gamaliel, on his status as a Roman citizen, or on his extensive knowledge of Scripture to accomplish his work (2 Corinthians 12:7; Philippians 3:3–8). He wrote to the Galatian church, "The life I now live in the body, I live *by faith* in the Son of God, who loved me and gave himself for me" (Galatians 2:20, emphasis added).

Paul knew that anything he accomplished of eternal importance would happen because God gave him the ability. He reminded the Corinthians, "What do you have that you did not receive? And if you did receive it, why do you boast as though you did not?" (1 Corinthians 4:7).

He not only relied on Christ, by faith, to empower him, but he understood why God had called him to do what he did—for God's glory, not his own.

Paul and, centuries later, Johann Sebastian Bach recognized that without God's enabling, they had no hope of creating anything worthwhile. Equally important, they recognized the pride-busting purpose of every Christian's existence—to bring God glory. *Soli Deo gloria.*

Embrace the Truth: Christians exist to glorify God, not ourselves.

Declare Your Faith: Lord, I believe I exist to glorify You. Everything I am and everything I do originates in You. Forgive me for the times I've tried to steal Your glory. Remind me, every day, to throw myself at Your feet to ask You to empower me. *Jesu juva.* And Lord, if I accomplish anything good, help me remember to give You the honor, glory, and praise. *Soli Deo gloria.* May my life point others to You. Amen.

I believe . . .

God is with me even in death

Even though I walk through the valley of the shadow of death, I will fear no evil, for you are with me.

Psalm 23:4 ESV

"Jim and I were married for fifty years," Marty said, her eyes shimmering with tears. "And now he was going somewhere I couldn't go—at least not yet. I couldn't take care of him anymore. What if dying was scary?" A tear slipped unnoticed out of the corner of her eye, leaving a silver trail down the side of her face.

"But then I remembered Lazarus and the rich man." She raised her eyes, and the slightest smile lifted the corners of her mouth. "Remember what happened when Lazarus died?" She clasped her hands together and tucked them under her chin. Lowering her voice and leaning toward me, she said, "Angels came and carried him to Abraham's side (Luke 16:22).

"Lazarus had lived most of his life alone, but he didn't die alone. God sent angels to take him from this world to the next." She paused a moment, lost in thought. "What if God did that for Jim? Wouldn't that be beautiful?" I nodded, imagining an angel escort tenderly carrying her beloved Jim into the presence of the Lord.

The Bible doesn't promise every believer an angelic escort into heaven, but it assures us that every death is holy. "Precious in the sight of the LORD is the death of his faithful servants," the psalmist wrote (Psalm 116:15). Even when we walk through the valley of the shadow of death, we need fear no evil, for God is with us (Psalm 23:4).

The apostle Paul declared, "I am convinced that neither death nor life, neither angels nor demons, neither the present nor the future, nor any powers, neither height nor depth, nor anything else in all creation, will be able to separate us from the love of God that is in Christ Jesus our Lord" (Romans 8:38–39).

When the cords of death entangle us, God doesn't leave us. He draws closer. When our bodies fail, and our souls separate from their earthly home, we enter the presence of the Lord (2 Corinthians 5:8).

Stephen, the church's first martyr, died at the hands of evil men. As his life ebbed away, he "looked up to heaven and saw the glory of God, and Jesus standing at the right hand of God. 'Look,' he said, 'I see heaven open and the Son of Man standing at the right hand of God'" (Acts 7:55–56). All other Scripture pictures Jesus seated at the right hand of the Father, but Stephen saw Jesus standing, eager to welcome His faithful son home.

Whether we're the one facing death or, like Marty, we're the one who's left behind, we need not fear. God is with us.

Embrace the Truth: Believers do not die alone. God is with us.

Declare Your Faith: Lord, I believe You will be with me even in death. Whether I die surrounded by a room full of loved ones or alone, You'll be there by my side. Because death is the portal to eternal life, I will not fear the process. You will carry me through. And then . . . oh my! What no eye has seen, what no ear has heard, and what no human mind has conceived—the things You have prepared for those who love You. Thank You, Father, for walking with me even through death to usher me into life eternal. I love You so much. Amen.

I believe . . .

God calls me to share what He's done for me

Come and hear, all you who fear God; let
me tell you what he has done for me.
Psalm 66:16

"I was lost. So lost."

No matter what topic my husband, David, speaks about, if he talks long enough, he'll mention how God saved him. He's been a bivocational pastor for most of his life, but whether he speaks from a pulpit or talks to a customer, he can't help sharing his gratitude and joy in Jesus.

My friend Jimmy's the same way.[9] "I lived most of my life imprisoned by sin and selfishness," he tells everyone who will listen. "Then God lifted me out of the mirey clay, set my feet upon a rock, and put a new song in my mouth. I promised Him I'd tell everyone I could what He's done for me."

And then there's Sadie. I know her testimony almost as well as I know my own because I've heard her share it so often. "I was a Christian," she says, "but I thought I had to earn God's love. No matter how hard I tried, I always fell short. During a terrible depression, God revealed Himself to me in ways I'd never experienced. My life changed forever. Now I know He loves me on my good days and on my bad ones."

David the psalmist would have loved to meet my David, Jimmy, and Sadie. Like them, he loved to brag about God and encourage others to do the same. In Psalm 66, he told his listeners, "Come and see what God has done, his awesome deeds for mankind!" (v. 5).

Then he challenged them, "Praise our God, all peoples, let the sound of his praise be heard" (v. 8).

He reminded them of God's marvelous acts on their behalf: "He has preserved our lives and kept our feet from slipping" (v. 9).

"Come and hear, all you who fear God," he proclaimed. "Let me tell you what he has done for me" (v. 16).

In this sixteenth verse, we see the key to winsome witnessing. It's not memorizing long passages of Scripture, learning a formal evangelism method, or committing an elaborate presentation to memory. It's telling others what God has done for us.

And the beauty of sharing our story? No one can argue with it.

An effective spiritual testimony has three parts: before, during, and after.

When my husband, David, taught the teens in our youth group how to share their testimonies, he said, "First, you share what your life was like before you placed your faith in Christ. Then you describe how you trusted Christ as your Savior. Finish up by telling them how your life is different now.

"You can't mess it up," he said. "It's your story. You know it well. Don't overthink it. Before, during, and after. You'll be amazed at how people respond."

I can see David the psalmist nodding from heaven and adding his amen to my David's encouragement.

"Come and hear, all you who fear God; let me tell you what he has done for me."

Embrace the Truth: God calls and enables every believer to share what He has done for us.

Declare Your Faith: Lord, I believe You're calling me to share my faith with those around me. I'm so grateful You saved me, and I want others to experience the joy and peace I have. I'd be lying if I didn't admit that talking about faith is scary. What if I mess it up? I want to be obedient. Help me see the opportunities You give me to tell of the marvelous things You've done in my life. Then give me the courage to open my mouth. Help me trust You for the results. In the strong name of Jesus I ask, amen.

I believe . . .

God calls me to love Him unconditionally

Jesus replied, "Love the Lord your God with all your heart and with all your soul and with all your mind."
Matthew 22:37

"Before God and these witnesses, I promise to love, honor, and cherish you, as long as you do everything my way, make sure my money doesn't run out, and give me everything I want."

Have you ever heard these words at a wedding ceremony? Of course not. Yet, without realizing it, I made this type of commitment to God. I felt loved by Him as long as He protected my family and me from sickness, heartache, trials, and grief. God revealed my flawed thinking during a family crisis. As best I could tell, I'd held up my end of the relationship—Bible reading, church attendance, giving, service. Yet my family was experiencing a season of great trial. Why?

Our time of testing revealed what I'd unknowingly believed—that if I did everything "right," God would protect me from hardship. I'd bought into the lie that the Christian life was a transactional relationship. If I did what I was supposed to do, God would do what He was supposed to do.

But God had "failed." My family was in shambles, and I felt hurt and disappointed.

Because I had built into my life the discipline of a morning Bible reading and prayer time, I continued to talk to God, even when the words I prayed were questioning and hurt filled. I brought my heartache to Him and sought His response in His Word.

Passages in the Bible reminded me how much God loved me. That He was good. Kind. Gentle. Wise. These truths bolstered my trust and reinforced my desire to cling to Him even when I didn't understand His ways. To love Him even when I didn't feel loved.

In the deepest point of my hurt, I drove a figurative faith stake into the ground using Job's holy words, "Though he slay me, yet will I hope in him" (Job 13:15).

"God, I don't understand why this is happening," I prayed, "but I don't have to understand to trust You."

Like a ship tossed in a hurricane, I had an anchor as the wind and waves continued to blow. God had allowed these circumstances for my good and His glory, and I could trust Him.

This declaration changed nothing about my circumstances, but it changed my heart. I knew that with God as my anchor, even when I drifted, He'd bring me back to Him.

Embrace the Truth: God—the all-faithful, trustworthy God—calls us to love Him unconditionally.

Declare Your Faith: Lord, I believe You call me to love You even when You allow hard circumstances in my life. I confess I'm tempted to pout, complain, or withhold my love from You when life doesn't go as I'd like. You don't deserve this. Considering what You did for me on the cross, You deserve my unconditional love—forever. Help me grow up in my faith and exercise unwavering trust in You. Amen.

I believe . . .

Jesus welcomes His children into His arms

When he had placed his hands on them . . .
Matthew 19:15

When my daughters were young, I read to them—a lot. Several times a day, we'd scoop up an armful of books and pile onto the couch, one daughter on one side and one daughter on the other. They'd press their little bodies into my sides and snuggle close—to see the pictures better, I assumed.

One day, I was cooking dinner when Mary Leigh, my three-year-old, bounced into the kitchen holding her favorite book. "Mommy, will you read to me?"

"I'm sorry, sweety, Mommy's cooking. But I bet Daddy will." With a nod and a smile, she bounced off as only a three-year-old girl can do. I saw them settle, side by side, on the couch. David opened the book and read,

"In an old house in Paris that was covered with vines, lived twelve little girls in two straight lines."[10] He'd barely finished the first page when Mary Leigh interrupted him.

"No, Daddy," she said with a frown. "You're not reading it right."

"What do you mean, I'm not reading it right?" He pointed, "It says right here, 'In an old house in Paris—'"

"No, Daddy," she said with an emphatic shake of her head, "You're *not* reading it right. You have to wrap around me."

She nudged his elbow up and wormed her way under his arm until she was snuggled close to his side.

"Ahhh," he said with a smile, "I have to wrap around you." He gave her a gentle squeeze, planted a kiss on her silky head, and began again. "In an old house in Paris that was covered with vines . . ."

Our daughter liked to be read to not only because she enjoyed hearing stories and looking at pictures but because she loved the feel of her father's embrace.

Perhaps this is why Jesus touched those He ministered to. A man born blind. A leper. Jairus's dead daughter. Mark 10:16 tells us He took children in His arms and blessed them.

Our precious daughter bore little resemblance to most of the people Jesus ministered to, but some days I look a lot like them. I blindly follow my path instead of Jesus. The leprosy of sin clings to me, destroying my witness and my fellowship with God. And I was dead in my sin before Christ extended to me His offer of grace.

In love and mercy He touched me. Not just a pat on the head or a kiss on the cheek. He stretched out His arms on the cross, then wrapped them around me and everyone who will believe in Him in a lavish display of life-giving, soul-cleansing forgiveness.

And, unlike my husband, Jesus never needs to be prompted. Every time we turn to Him, He opens His arms and welcomes us into His embrace.

Embrace the Truth: Jesus eagerly wraps His loving arms around His children.

Declare Your Faith: Lord, I believe You're not only willing to draw close to me, You eagerly welcome me into Your arms. On good days I feel comfortable coming to You in prayer and fellowship. On bad days, when I disappoint myself and You, I find Your loving welcome hard to believe. And yet it's true. Every time I turn to You, You wrap around me. I love You so much.

I believe . . .

If I resist the devil, he will flee

Submit yourselves, then, to God. Resist the devil, and he will flee from you.

James 4:7

How often do you think about the devil? The real devil—not the mean coworker in the next cubicle—the serpent in the garden of Eden, Lucifer, Satan.

Some Christians see the him everywhere. They assume he's all-powerful and irresistible. They credit him with every temptation they face, even the ones that they knowingly walk into, and assume they're doomed once he trains his sights on them.

The rest of us, if we're honest, don't think much about him. We might credit him with a particularly heinous crime, but since he's a created being and can only be in one place at one time, we assume we're not important enough for him to bother with us.

Au contraire.

Satan himself may not have us in his sights, but his influence has the power to destroy us. Paul reminded the Ephesians, "For our struggle is not against flesh and blood, but against the rulers, against the authorities, against the powers of this dark world and against the spiritual forces of evil in the heavenly realms" (6:12).

Satan and his influencers are real, but they're not all-powerful. They can't read our minds, but they can read our behavior. Like a football coach who studies the opponent's game films, they've been looking for gaps in humanity's defenses since Eden. James

1:14 reveals that our own evil desires cause most of our sin, but the devil knows how to exploit these desires.

Do believers have any hope of vanquishing such a formidable enemy, one Peter described as a prowling lion seeking his next meal (1 Peter 5:8)?

We do! James tells us how: "Submit yourselves, then, to God. Resist the devil, and he will flee from you" (4:7).

First, submit to God.

The verb *to submit* "was a Greek military term meaning 'to arrange [troop divisions] in a military fashion under the command of a leader.' In non-military use, it was 'a voluntary attitude of giving in [and] cooperating.'"[11]

When we willingly submit ourselves to God, we acknowledge His way is best. We eagerly align our beliefs, actions, and attitudes to what He has revealed in the Bible. This helps us recognize and avoid Satan's traps.

Sometimes, though, a submissive heart isn't enough. On days when Satan's influence launches a full on, frontal assault, we must employ the second step of James's strategy: "Resist the devil." To *resist* is another military term that means "to take a stand."[12]

As Puritan pastor and author Thomas Manton reminds us,

> The devil cannot force you, he can only try to persuade you.
>
> He is like a dog that stands looking and waving his tail ready to receive something from those who sit at the table; but if nothing is thrown to him—an angry word; an unclean glance; gestures of wrath and discontent—without any of that being thrown to him by those seated at the table, he goes away.[13]

Herein lies the glorious power that believers have—the power to take a stand and refuse to do what the devil is tempting us to do.

When we resist, he gives up. Picture this glorious sight.

Would you like to gain victory over Satan's tricks and temptations? You know what to do. Submit and resist.

Then watch the devil and his influencers run.

Embrace the Truth: Believers possess the power to resist the devil and make him flee.

Declare Your Faith: Father, I believe, through the Holy Spirit's power within me, I can resist Satan's tricks and temptations. Help me, each day, to submit myself to Your direction and obey Your Word. Give me eyes to see Satan's lies and not fall prey to his schemes. Thank you that I already have the power to resist him, through Jesus Christ who lives in me. Amen.

I believe . . .

God protects me through the local church

Brothers and sisters, if someone is caught in a sin, you who live by the Spirit should restore that person gently.

Galatians 6:1

As we gathered in the tiny church kitchen after our monthly potluck dinner, Mike, one of our deacons, made a surprising offer.

"I'll wash if someone else will dry."

The church kitchen doesn't have a dishwasher, so members usually take turns washing the serving plates and utensils after a meal. Mike had never volunteered to help wash before, but we didn't expect him to.

He was blind.

"You sure, Mike?" I said.

"Yep. As long as someone goes behind me to inspect, I'm pretty good at washing dishes."

And he was.

Mike relies on his sense of touch to "see" what his eyes can't. As he scrubbed a casserole dish edged with baked-on sweet potato, he knew exactly where the sticky spots were. The pie pan with the grooved edges, however, gave him a little more trouble.

"Did I get everything?" he said, holding up the pan.

"Almost." I took the dish from him and rubbed a stubborn spot with a cloth.

I'm fully sighted (if you allow for the contact lenses I wear to help me see distance), but even I miss stuff. My husband pulled a dish out of our kitchen cupboard recently that still had oatmeal clinging to the rim. Maybe I'd been in a hurry the morning I washed it, or careless. Back into the sink it went.

Mike and I need others to help us see the dishwashing errors we're blind to. We need help in our spiritual lives too. When we're sucked into a sinful habit or harmful behavior, we're often blind to its hold on us. If we realize it, we sometimes downplay its seriousness.

Thankfully, God made provision for our spiritual blindness by placing us in a body of believers and giving them permission to speak into our lives.

"Brothers and sisters," Paul wrote to the church at Galatia, "if someone is caught in a sin, you who live by the Spirit should restore that person gently" (Galatians 6:1).

The apostle James gave similar encouragement. "If one of you should wander from the truth and someone should bring that person back, remember this: Whoever turns a sinner from the error of their way will save them from death and cover over a multitude of sins" (James 5:19–20).

Within the accountability and relationships of the local church, God has provided a safety net to keep us from falling into sin-infested waters. Christians who "can be a Christian without going to church" or "can worship God just as well from my living room" deprive themselves of the protection they need to live a godly life.

Solomon said it best: "Two are better than one, because they have a good return for their labor: If either of them falls down, one can help the other up. But pity anyone who falls and has no one to help them up" (Ecclesiastes 4:9–10). Whether we're washing dishes or walking in faith, I'm glad God has a plan in place.

Embrace the Truth: God provides brothers and sisters within the body of Christ to warn and protect us.

Declare Your Faith: Lord, I believe Your plan to protect me from sin includes accountability within the church, the body of

Christ. Forgive me for the times I've disparaged or devalued the importance of the church in my life. Help me love the church as You do and make every effort to actively participate. Enable me to build deep relationships with my brothers and sisters in Christ that will allow us to speak words of edification, correction, and compassion to each other. Give me courage to speak words of warning when necessary and receive those same words when I wander away. In the strong name of Jesus I ask, amen.

I believe . . .

I must recognize I'm lost to be saved

I have not come to call the righteous, but sinners to repentance.
Luke 5:32

I watched the family sitting across from me in a restaurant and tried to not laugh. Mom, Dad, two older siblings, and a wide-eyed, tousle-haired toddler—the birthday boy.

His three-year-old friends, with parents in tow, joined them soon after. They demolished three large pizzas, then played games, opened presents, and ate cake. Chocolate cake. Chocolate cake with lots of squishy frosting.

It was obvious the birthday boy loved cake. By the time he had finished his piece, icing covered his cheeks, his nose, and his hands. Cake crumbs dotted with frosting and sprinkles stuck to his hair. A brown smear, like a third eyebrow, decorated his forehead.

"Here buddy," his dad said, "let me clean your face." He rested his hand on the boy's head and reached for a napkin.

Empowered, perhaps, by his new status as a three-year-old, the birthday boy blocked his father's attempt to clean his face.

"No," he said. "Me do it."

Grabbing the napkin from his father, he scrubbed at his chocolate-covered cheeks, smearing the icing, and making more of a mess than when he began.

Pleased and proud, he handed the sticky napkin to his father and announced, "I done."

I was once this little boy. Only I was eighteen, not three (and a girl, of course).

Riding the celebration train of high school graduation, I reveled in all I was—fourth in my graduating class, a faithful church goer, winner of a full-tuition scholarship to the college of my choice. A "good girl" who worked hard, (mostly) obeyed her parents, and respected her elders. When I thought about God, which wasn't often, I assumed He appreciated my positive contribution to the world. As far as I was concerned, my face was clean.

From God's perspective, I was smeared with selfishness, half-truths, and immorality. I served others only when it served my purposes. I vacillated between fear and pride.

But these weren't sins, I rationalized. Sins were murder, theft, and adultery, not "personality quirks" or "indiscretions." Surely the good works wipe away the other stuff.

I'm forever grateful for the day my heavenly Father held the mirror of His perfect standard (Matthew 5:48) up to my sin-slathered self. He helped me recognize my sin for what it really was and said, "Let me clean your face."

I discovered, along with believers down through the ages, that the only way to be saved is to recognize we are lost.

Paul describes it this way: "At one time we too were foolish, disobedient, deceived and enslaved by all kinds of passions and pleasures. We lived in malice and envy, being hated and hating one another. But when the kindness and love of God our Savior appeared, he saved us, not because of righteous things we had done, but because of his mercy. He saved us through the washing of rebirth and renewal by the Holy Spirit" (Titus 3:3–5).

Salvation is a bit more complicated than wiping frosting off a toddler's face, but when we see our need in the mirror of God's Word, we've taken a very important first step.

Embrace the Truth: The only way to be saved is to recognize we are lost.

Declare Your Faith: Lord, I believe I was lost—so lost—before You saved me. All my good works are nothing but filthy rags compared to Your perfect holiness. Forgive me for trying to cobble together my own good works instead of resting in the good work You did on the cross on my behalf. Clean me up, Lord, by washing my sins away with the water of Your forgiveness. Make me more like Jesus. Amen.

I believe . . .

God calls me to study His Word

Do your best to present yourself to God as one approved, a worker who does not need to be ashamed and who correctly handles the word of truth.

2 Timothy 2:15

"I just want to be happy," Sophia said.

Kat, a petite brunette with freckles sprinkled across her nose, nodded. "And wise. I'd love to know what to do in every situation. Life is so confusing."

Jaqui sighed, propped her elbow on the table, and cradled her chin in her hand. "I've done so many dumb things in my life. I'd love to put them all behind me and start over."

Lily loved the group of young women who met with her every Monday night in the coffee shop. They'd studied together since the girls were college freshmen. Now they were in their last semester of school. Soon they'd graduate and head out into the world.

More than ever, Lily felt the press of time prompting her to speak frankly.

"Girls, I have good news. You can have all these things—and more."

Now she had their attention. She opened her Bible, flipped a few pages, and said, "Listen to what King David wrote in Psalm 19:

> The law of the Lord is perfect,
> refreshing the soul.

The statutes of the Lord are trustworthy,
making wise the simple.
The precepts of the Lord are right,
giving joy to the heart.
The commands of the Lord are radiant,
giving light to the eyes.
The fear of the Lord is pure,
enduring forever.
The decrees of the Lord are firm,
and all of them are righteous.

They are more precious than gold,
than much pure gold;
they are sweeter than honey,
than honey from the honeycomb.
(vv. 7–10)

"If we want reviving, wisdom, joy, endurance, an understanding of right and wrong, and something better than money or food"—Lily raised her Bible—"we're holding the key in our hands."

Like Lily with "her girls," Paul the aged apostle had a young protegee. His "son in the faith," Timothy, had served beside him since his youth and now pastored the church of Ephesus. Timothy wasn't on the verge of graduating, but Paul might have been. He knew his imprisonment could end in death and sensed the time of his departure was at hand.

His letters to Timothy brim with truth and instruction. He shared the key to dynamic Christian living in 2 Timothy 2:15: "Do your best to present yourself to God as one approved, a worker who does not need to be ashamed and who correctly handles the word of truth."

"God's Word is the source of life, hope, help, and transformation," Lily told her girls. "But we can't just carry it back and forth to church on Sunday and expect miracles. We have to read and study it. Work to understand it. Ask God to help us live it out.

When we do, He'll make us wise. We'll discover our purpose, find direction, and experience true joy.

"Best of all," she said, eyes bright with conviction, "we'll learn how amazingly wonderful God is. Once we grasp this, we'll trust Him with everything.

"Now," she said, "let's open our Bibles and see what God has for us today."

Embrace the Truth: God's call to study His Word leads to joy, peace, and transformation.

Declare Your Faith: Lord, I believe You call all Christians, not just seminarians and pastors, to study the Bible. Give me a hunger not just to read it but to dig deeply, study broadly, and apply what You show me to my everyday life. Guide me to excellent resources and solid teachers, but remind me first and foremost to ask the Holy Spirit to be my teacher. Help me not only to study the Word but to obey what it says. Amen.

I believe . . .

God calls me to not complain

Do everything without grumbling or arguing, so that you may become blameless and pure, "children of God without fault in a warped and crooked generation." Then you will shine among them like stars in the sky.

Philippians 2:14–15

"If you want to be a better witness, quit complaining."

I remembered my pastor's words as I stood in a long line at the grocery store. Whether they were shorthanded or all the cashiers but one chose the five o'clock hour to go on break, I couldn't tell. What I could tell was that the one remaining cashier was about to lose it.

In front of me, a woman huffed loudly enough for everyone to hear. "This line is five people deep. Why have all these registers if they're not going to staff them? I don't have time for this. My ice cream's going to melt before I get out of the store."

Her friend said something soothing, but her gentle tone did little to quiet her companion.

"Why is it so hot in here?" the woman said, fanning herself with a store circular. "Don't they know it's July? My makeup's going to be as melted as my ice cream." She dabbed her hairline with the back of her hand and fanned harder. "Remind me never to shop here again. It's just not worth it to save a few pennies."

When her turn finally came, she had a few words for the cashier.

"Honey, y'all just gotta do a better job. You can't make people wait like this. You're gonna lose customers, and then you won't have a job." She plopped her oversize purse on the counter and swiped her card.

Leaving the receipt in the cashier's hand, she grabbed her ice cream and headed for the door. I heard her voice one more time before she disappeared.

"Have a blessed day!"

If Grumpy Gilda was a Christian, she might have benefited from Pastor Tim's teaching and the apostle Paul's instruction from the book of Philippians.

"Do everything without grumbling or arguing, so that you may become blameless and pure, 'children of God without fault in a warped and crooked generation.' Then you will shine among them like stars in the sky" (Philippians 2:14–15).

"Would you like to be a witness to the 'warped and crooked' generation we live in?" Pastor Tim asked us that Wednesday night. "Then quit complaining. If you refuse to join in the negativity, your attitude will be so different people will want to know why. Then you can point 'em to Jesus."

Until that evening, I'd always considered the tendency to complain as more of a personality type than a sin. But there it was in black and white: a command to not complain—and a promise. If I do everything without complaining, I can become blameless (of a critical and ungrateful spirit) and pure in my interactions with others. Then I'll shine like a joy-filled witness in our dark world.

Isn't this what we hope to do? "Let your light shine before others," Jesus said to His disciples, "that they may see your good deeds and glorify your Father in heaven" (Matthew 5:16).

Unlike Gilda, I do plan to shop at that grocery store again. And if I have to wait in line? With God's help, I want to wait without grumbling. Maybe then I'll shine for Jesus.

Embrace the Truth: Refusing to complain will help us stand out as a testimony to the transforming power of Jesus.

Declare Your Faith: Lord, I believe You call me to respond to irritations without complaining. I want to be a shining witness to those I encounter, and if choosing to not complain will set me apart, then by God's grace, I'll do it. But You have to help me. This doesn't come naturally. When I'm tempted to complain, set a guard over my lips and fill my mouth with gratitude instead of grumbling. In the strong name of Jesus I ask, amen.

I believe . . .

God takes no pleasure in the death of the wicked

As surely as I live, declares the Sovereign Lord,
I take no pleasure in the death of the wicked,
but rather that they turn from their ways and
live. Turn! Turn from your evil ways!

Ezekiel 33:11

I suspect, for every person who loves the Old Testament, there are many who hate it. I spoke to one such person recently.

"I read the Old Testament once," she said. "Page after page of fire and brimstone. Entire books devoted to the horrible things God was going to do to people. Locust plagues, famine, conquering nations. If this is how God deals with people, I don't want to have anything to do with Him. I prefer a God of love."

I do too. And we don't have to look beyond the Old Testament to find Him. Contrary to what the woman I spoke with thought, the Old Testament gives us innumerable glimpses of God's loving heart.

From Genesis to Malachi, we see how He pursues people, opens their eyes to their sinfulness and their need for a Savior, and extends His glorious and gracious offer of salvation to all who will believe.

Many assume salvation began in the New Testament with Jesus, but it began at the dawn of time. God created humanity with the ability to have a relationship with Him. Then He called one man, Abraham, to become the father of the nation of Israel, a family set apart for His purposes.

But He didn't limit His love to the Jews. He extended His offer of salvation to all who would believe. Some did.

Most didn't. They remained in their sin, willfully disregarding the magnificent displays of power God provided so "you will know that I am the LORD" (Exodus 7:17).

Yet God continued to reveal Himself to Jew and Gentile alike. For *thousands* of years, He reached out to mankind, withheld His judgment, and extended His grace. A close reading of the Old Testament reveals that every threat of punishment came only after He called people, multiple times, to repent and be reconciled.

Listen to His plea to the Israelites and you'll hear His heart for all people: "As surely as I live, declares the Sovereign LORD, I take no pleasure in the death of the wicked, but rather that they turn from their ways and live. Turn! Turn from your evil ways! Why will you die?" (Ezekiel 33:11).

God is holy and deserves our worship, honor, and obedience. Because He's holy, He can't ignore sin. But in His mercy, He pleads with humanity to turn from our wicked ways and live.

This is the God of the Old Testament and the God of the New—a God who takes no pleasure in the death of the wicked.

He loves us. From eternity past to eternity future, He extends His grace to all who will believe.

Embrace the Truth: God isn't a vengeful God who enjoys punishing humanity. He's a loving God who longs for all who will believe to come to Him.

Declare Your Faith: Lord, I believe You take no pleasure in punishing the wicked. As Jesus said when He wept over Jerusalem, You long to gather people in Your arms as a hen gathers her chicks, but they won't let You. Thank You for Your patience and willingness to continue to call people to Yourself. Thank You for pursuing the lost with lovingkindness and mercy. Please, oh Lord, extend Your mercy to those I love and save them. In the strong name of Jesus I ask, amen.

I believe . . .

God loves me

I pray that you, being rooted and established in love, may have power, together with all the Lord's holy people, to grasp how wide and long and high and deep is the love of Christ.

Ephesians 3:17–18

To become a parent is to "decide forever to have your heart go walking around outside your body."[14]

Someone shared these poignant words with me at a baby shower, when I was expecting my first daughter. I nodded and smiled, but I had no idea how pregnant with truth the saying is. A month away from delivering, I'd been experiencing sleep disturbances, Braxton Hicks contractions, and sciatic nerve pain. Indigestion, shortness of breath, and leg cramps. The thought of my baby living outside my body sounded delightful, not troubling.

Little did I know that one day I'd wish I knew exactly where she was, what she was doing, and, most of all, that she was safe from harm.

As my daughter grew, and then my second daughter, they became increasingly independent. They went places without me. Learned from people I didn't know. Made decisions without my input. In time they moved away and married.

With every new location and life change, I've visited them. Washington, Lynchburg, Roanoke, Alexandria, Yokosuka, Rota, and Seattle. I love my daughters, and if my heart's going to go walking around outside my body, I want to know where it's going.

Some days the love I feel toward my girls presses against the walls of my chest until it aches—physically, emotionally, and spiritually. Yet as powerful as this love is, it's flawed and frail. Some days it's selfish. Other days it's lazy. Because it lives in my redeemed-yet-still-sinful heart, it has human limitations.

Not so with God's love. Unlike human love, which has physical barriers and the limitations of time and distance, divine love knows no bounds. It surrounds us when we lie down and when we awaken (Psalm 139:18).

God has engraved us on the palms of His hands and ever lives to make intercession for us. (Isaiah 49:16; Hebrews 7:25). He laid down His life for us (1 John 3:16) and promises never to forsake us (Hebrews 13:5). Even when we are faithless, He is faithful (2 Timothy 2:13).

As a Father to the fatherless (Psalm 68:5) and a bridegroom to His bride (Mark 2:19), God provides for and protects us. His covenant love follows us to the ends of the earth and the end of our lives (Jeremiah 31:3; Isaiah 46:4).

Parenthood has given me glimpses of the magnitude of the love God has for me—and for you. Eternity will prove the depths of it.

Embrace the Truth: Human love can't compare to the depths of God's love for me.

Declare Your Faith: Lord, I believe You love me—even when I don't feel lovable. You showed Your love by dying on the cross, and You've been faithful to me all my life. On the basis of Your actions and Your Word, I choose to believe this. When my emotions or my circumstances tempt me to think otherwise, help me remind myself that feelings lie, but You never do. Thank You for loving me. I can't wait to hug You on that glorious day when my faith becomes sight.

I believe . . .

God's people must be kind and gentle

The Lord's servant must not be quarrelsome but must be kind to everyone, able to teach, not resentful.

2 Timothy 2:24

Marge loves Jesus, other people, and her country. When she listens to the news or online commentators, she often grows discouraged. She worries about the world her grandchildren will inherit, one that seems to have no room for God.

Sometimes Marge's sadness about the state of the world, the nation, and the church morphs into anger. She talks back to the television and calls out the politicians and spokespersons who promote a non-Christian philosophy.

Occasionally, Marge shares her thoughts with flesh-and-blood people—loudly.

"I'm passionate about the truth," she said as we sat in her kitchen sipping tea. "And when I get passionate, I get loud." She described a conversation she had with a family member.

"He was spouting off something crazy, so I asked him, 'How can you believe that nonsense?' Then I told him what the Bible said." A sheepish look crossed her face. "Unfortunately, the more we 'discussed' things, the louder we got, until before long we were shouting at each other."

"It was downhill from there," Marge said glumly. "Now we're not speaking." She met my eyes, and I saw a flicker of regret. "All I wanted to do was share the truth."

If Paul had been sitting with us in Marge's kitchen that day, he might have given her the same advice he gave Timothy, his beloved son in the faith.

"The Lord's servant must not be quarrelsome but must be kind to everyone, able to teach, not resentful. Opponents must be gently instructed, in the hope that God will grant them repentance leading them to a knowledge of the truth" (2 Timothy 2:24–25).

As a young pastor, Timothy interacted with false teachers, confused church members, and unbelievers. His calling required him to defend the gospel against false teaching and proclaim Jesus as the only way to heaven. As he counseled those under his care, Timothy needed to learn to speak the truth gently and in love.

Paul knew angry voices didn't advance the cause of Christ. That quarrelsome words and arrogant tones drive people away from the truth, not toward it.

Gentle tones, in contrast, create space for questions and dialogue. They invite conversation. A respectful exchange of ideas, with equal parts listening and talking, leaves room for the Holy Spirit to work.

Spiritual conversations done kindly can ferry an unbeliever across the bay of false thinking into the harbor of truth—the kind of truth that leads to salvation.

"The next time I feel that passion burning in my heart," Marge said, "I'm going to take a deep breath and ask God to fill my mouth with gentle words."

"Passionately gentle," I said with a laugh.

And Marge laughed too.

Embrace the Truth: God uses the gentleness and kindness of His servants to lead unbelievers to the truth.

Declare Your Faith: Lord, I believe You call me to treat people kindly and with gentleness. This is the way Jesus acted toward unbelievers, and You call me to imitate Him. Forgive me when I respond in anger or arrogance. I know anger never accomplishes

Your purposes (James 1:20). Fill my mouth with gentle, grace-filled words. I want to be an instrument in Your hand to lead people to the truth and, ultimately, to repentance and faith in You. Be glorified through the words I speak. Amen.

I believe . . .

My heart will deceive me

Trust in the LORD with all your heart and lean not on your own understanding; in all your ways submit to him, and he will make your paths straight.

Proverbs 3:5–6

"I knew what my parents had taught me," Tessa said, "and I knew what the Bible said, but I was in love. Somehow, in my mind at least, that made it all right." She flipped her long, dark hair over her shoulder and continued. "I was a sophomore, and he was a senior. I couldn't believe he was interested in me. And he was cute—really cute."

I'd heard the story before, but the girls in our disciple group hadn't.

"By Christmas we were exclusive. My head said we were moving too fast, but my heart was thrilled. I loved him so much. And he loved me."

She crossed her arms and made eye contact with several of the girls sitting closest to her. "But you know what? Sometimes your heart lies. And takes you places you shouldn't go.

"Before long, I was sneaking out to see him. Lying to my parents. I'd tell 'em I was hanging out with a friend, but I was with him." She leaned forward, rested her elbows on her knees, and clasped her hands.

"Telling my mom and dad I was pregnant was the second hardest thing I've ever done in my life." She looked down at the floor, remembering. When she raised her head, tears shimmered in her eyes. "Giving up my baby for adoption was the first."

"I've discovered you usually regret following your heart," she said with a sad smile, "but you never regret following God."

Tessa discovered what we all must learn—that we can't trust our hearts. Following our heart will take us places we never intended to go, will make us do things we never dreamed we'd do, and will cause more grief than we ever imagined we'd experience.

The prophet Jeremiah wasn't exaggerating when he said, "The heart is deceitful above all things, and desperately sick; who can understand it?" (Jeremiah 17:9 ESV) Our heart is a tyrant screaming for what it wants, regardless of the cost. Apart from God's sanctifying work, it's a restless evil, bent on satisfying every selfish pleasure it can dream up. It's the incubator of thoughts and actions that destroy our homes, our churches, and our lives.

Jesus warned, "Out of the heart come evil thoughts—murder, adultery, sexual immorality, theft, false testimony, slander" (Matthew 15:19). My heart often entertains fear, selfishness, and unforgiveness.

But believers have an alternative to trusting our heart. "Trust in the LORD with all your heart and lean not on your own understanding; in all your ways submit to him, and he will make your paths straight" (Proverbs 3:5–6).

King David, whose heart led him to commit adultery and murder, confessed his sin and prayed, "Create in me a pure heart, O God, and renew a steadfast spirit within me" (Psalm 51:10). We, too, can ask God to make our hearts pure and surrendered to Him.

When Jesus's disciples felt anxious, He counseled them, "Do not let your hearts be troubled. You believe in God; believe also in me" (John 14:1). It was His way of saying, "If you listen to your heart, you'll feel afraid. If you listen to God, you'll experience peace."

If we follow the Good Shepherd instead of our hearts, He promises to lead us in "paths of righteousness for his name's sake" (Psalm 23:3 ESV). He'll fill our cups to overflowing—without the pain of regret. And He'll surround us with goodness and mercy all the days of our lives.

As Tessa so eloquently said, we usually regret following our hearts, but we'll never regret following our Savior.

Embrace the Truth: My heart will deceive me, but God never will.

Declare Your Faith: Lord, I believe my heart will deceive me. I know it has. It's lied to me about what will make me happy and what's best for me. My heart has told me I should trust my feelings, even when they contradict Your Word. I don't want to be ruled by my feelings. I want to be led by You. Help me seek Your wisdom every day in prayer and in Your Word. Amen.

I believe . . .

The gospel has the power to save

I am not ashamed of the gospel, because it is the power of God that brings salvation to everyone who believes.

Romans 1:16

Dr. Wall made some incredible promises that day.

"If you surrender your life to Christ," my pastor said, his voice deep with conviction, "He'll come to live inside you. He'll forgive your sins, change your desires, and, one day, take you to heaven to live with Him forever."

Jesus living inside me? Forgiveness for everything I'd ever said, done, and thought? A mind-and-heart-altering transformation? And a home in heaven one day? Wow! Way more than I'd hoped for when I dragged my miserable self into his office and poured out my anxious heart.

Now, more than forty years later, I can say with confidence, everything he said was true. Not only for me, but for everyone who has placed their faith in the gospel of Jesus Christ. As the apostle Paul wrote in his letter to the Romans, the gospel truly is "the power of God that brings salvation to everyone who believes" (v. 16).

How do I know this? First and foremost, because the Bible says so. It's God's declared Word, and it's filled with stunning examples of transformed lives and hearts. Saul, the religious zealot who once hunted down, jailed, and executed Christians, was so powerfully transformed that he evangelized most of the known world and wrote a large portion of the New Testament. Peter the fisherman went from denying Jesus to defending Him. When he was beaten and thrown into jail for sharing the gospel, he rejoiced because he was counted worthy to suffer for Christ.

In modern days, the power of the gospel transformed C. S. Lewis, Josh McDowell, and Lee Strobel from intellectual skeptics into fierce defenders of the faith.

And then there's me. Before I surrendered my life to Christ, I was fearful, selfish, and self-centered. Everything revolved around me—what I wanted, what best served my interests, and what would make me happy. Then, by God's good grace, He saved me and began a transformation that continues today. Sometimes I'm still fearful, selfish, and self-centered, but, little by little, God is changing me to act and think more like Jesus.

When I grow fearful, I pray. When I'm tempted to keep God's gifts to myself, I remember His generous heart toward me. When I forget that my purpose in life is to help build God's kingdom, not my own, the Holy Spirit gently nudges me back to this higher purpose.

God's Word declares that the gospel has the power to save and transform. History and my life testify to this truth. I hope your life does too.

If you haven't personally experienced the power of the gospel, today can be the day.

Confess, repent, and believe.*

Then marvel at what happens next.

Embrace the Truth: Lord, I believe that the truth of the gospel—Jesus died, was buried, and rose again—has the power to save everyone who believes.

Declare Your Faith: Thank You, precious Jesus, for dying on the cross to save us. I'm so grateful we don't have to wait for heaven to

* For a detailed explanation of the gospel and a sample prayer, turn to "How to Have a Relationship with Christ" on page 165.

experience the salvation and transformation You promise. When fear or insecurity tempts me to keep the gospel to myself, remind me that it's Your power, not mine, that will bring salvation to all who believe. In the strong name of Jesus I ask, amen.

I believe . . .

Jesus prayed for me

I pray also for those who will believe
in me through their message.
John 17:20

When my friend Terri was dying, she seldom talked about herself. "I know I'll be with Jesus," she said once. "I'm not afraid." But she talked about her loved ones a lot—her husband, her sisters, her children: What will happen to them when I'm gone? How will they cope with my death? Who will take care of them?

I find it especially tender that on the night before Jesus's death, He, too, was thinking about His loved ones—His beloved disciples. The men who had pledged their lives to Him.

He knew they'd struggle when He was gone. They'd wrestle with the horror of His death. They'd need someone to guide, provide for, and protect them. So He prayed for them. John recorded this prayer in John 17:6–19.

But this isn't all John recorded. He captured another prayer, one that reveals who else Jesus had on His heart that fateful night. After He finished praying for His disciples, Jesus prayed for us—for you and for me and for all the believers who would place their faith in Him.

On the night before He was crucified, knowing full well the horror and pain that awaited Him, Jesus was thinking about and praying *for us.*

He asked God to knit us together with other believers so we could enjoy the tender oneness He enjoyed with His Father (v. 21). To make us perfect in this unity and use our unity as a witness, that "the world will know that you sent me and have loved them even as you have loved me" (v. 23).

"Father," He prayed, "I want those you have given me to be with me where I am, and to see my glory, the glory you have given me because you loved me before the creation of the world" (v. 24). Take 'em to heaven one day, Father. Let them see me—not as a man with dusty feet and a tired body but as a radiant Savior in all my glory.

"[May] the love you have for me . . . be in them, and that I myself may be in them," He asked (v. 26). Fill them up, precious Father, with the same love with which You love me.

As my friend Terri prepared to die, she thought of her loved ones. She asked God to care for them, meet their needs, and draw them close to Himself.

On the night Jesus died, He thought of us—of you, of me, and of all who will believe in His name.

And He prayed for us.

How does this make you feel? Think on this today.

Embrace the Truth: On the night before Jesus died, He prayed for you.

Declare Your Faith: Precious Jesus, I believe You loved me enough to pray for me on the night before Your crucifixion. And I believe God heard You. Thank You for thinking of me on one of the darkest nights of Your earthly life. Whenever I feel alone, abandoned, or unloved, remind me of this.

I believe . . .

God will draw near to me

Draw near to God, and he will draw near to you.
James 4:8 ESV

"Hi, Andrew," I said as I entered the dining room where my five-year-old grandson sat, "can I have a hug?" His forehead scrunched in concentration as he snapped Lego blocks together, but as I drew near, he hopped down from his chair and raced toward me.

"Gigi!" he said, as he flung himself into my arms. He wrapped me in a hug, squeezed as only a five-year-old boy can squeeze, laid his head on my chest and snuggled close. "I'm glad you're here." Legos forgotten, we sat together laughing, talking, and enjoying each other's presence.

Snuggling with a child is one of the sweetest joys in life, but it's nothing compared with the joy of approaching God and finding His arms open wide.

I don't have unlimited access to Andrew and my other grandkids. Time, distance, and responsibilities limit the time we spend together. But I have twenty-four-hour access to God my Father. The sweet promise of James 4:8 describes how to enter into His presence: "Draw near to God, and he will draw near to you" (ESV).

We don't have to be the biggest donor at our church, volunteer for hours at the neighborhood soup kitchen, or deny ourselves food or pleasure to earn an audience with God. We don't have to learn how to pronounce grandiose words like *propitiation* and *sanctification* or be able to list the books of the Old and New Testament to be deemed worthy of His notice.

We just have to draw near.

But it takes effort on our part. Andrew and I wouldn't have enjoyed our sweet time together if I'd remained on the porch. Or stood aloof, with my arms crossed in the corner of the room. I had to come near.

So it is with God. While He is often the initiator in our relationship (He drew us to Himself in salvation and convicts us of sin), He'll never force His closeness on us. He waits for us to turn our hearts toward Him.

But when we do—oh, glorious thought—He draws near.

Every single time.

Have you ever reached out to someone, and they shunned you? You offered them friendship or companionship, and they said, "No, thanks"? Shared your heart, but they didn't reciprocate?

God will never do this.

Every time we draw near to Him, He opens His arms wide and pulls us close. He listens, empathizes, and encourages. Whether we choose to spend a minute, an hour, or a day with Him, He lingers. The conversation ends only when we walk away.

And when we draw near again? He draws near again too.

If you're feeling distant from God today, take that first step. Draw near to Him in prayer or Bible reading. He will draw near to you.

He promised.

Embrace the Truth: Every time we draw near to God, He opens His arms wide and pulls us close.

Declare Your Faith: Lord, I believe You respond to every move I make toward You. Thank You for being a responsive Father who's never too busy to draw near. Help me resist the tendency to think I'm too busy (or too self-sufficient) to need a daily, hourly, moment-by-moment awareness of Your presence. I love You so much.

I believe . . .

God promises I'll spend eternity with Him

These words are trustworthy and true.
Revelation 22:6

Annie was so sick. Eighteen months of chemo had robbed her of her hair, her eyebrows, her weight, and her energy. Most days she had the will to fight—to do whatever it took to slay the beast that threatened to take her life. Other days she wanted to quit.

Today was one of those days.

The cumulative effects of the toxic chemicals that dripped into her veins every two weeks had worn her down. Everything she ate (when she felt like eating, which wasn't often), tasted metallic. Nausea clung to her, sometimes awakening her in the middle of the night with its violent waves. Walking to the next room or down the hall seemed as impossible as paddling around the world in a kayak.

"I don't think I can do this anymore," she whispered to her husband, Sam, as he helped her dress.

"You can, honey," he said. "Only four more treatments."

Tears slid down her sunken cheeks as she shook her head.

"Remember what's waiting for you at the end of all this. Remember what I promised you?"

Annie smiled for the first time that morning. "Alaska."

"Alaska," Sam nodded. "We'll take a helicopter ride to a glacier, see the Northern Lights—and chase whales. You've always wanted to see a whale, and there are lots of them in Alaska."

Annie smiled again, nodding.

"And you'll eat all that delicious food without feeling queasy. You'll gain so much weight we'll have to roll you off the ship."

She laughed at the thought, so far removed from their current reality.

When Annie's spirits sagged and her hope dwindled, Sam reminded her of the cruise he'd promised. He knew that without hope, Annie couldn't endure the dark days of her cancer treatment.

John the apostle wasn't going through cancer treatments, but he was suffering trials of his own. Scripture tells us that, as an aged man, he had been banished to the isle of Patmos for his faith. History fills in the horrifying details. Prior to his exile, it's believed his captors had boiled him in oil to try to end his life.[15]

How fitting that God gave John, a man clinging to faith and serving God to the end, a glorious glimpse of what he had to look forward to—what God has promised for those who believe. God lifted his eyes from his painful present to his—and our—glorious future.

"Then I saw 'a new heaven and a new earth,'" John wrote, "for the first heaven and the first earth had passed away. . . . I saw the Holy City, the new Jerusalem, coming down out of heaven from God, prepared as a bride beautifully dressed for her husband" (Revelation 21:1–2).

Golden streets, sparkling rivers, and a banquet table laden with delicacies.

"'There will be no more death' or mourning or crying or pain, for the old order of things has passed away" (v. 4).

No cancer. No chemo. No funerals.

And best of all?

God will be there.

"And I heard a loud voice from the throne saying, 'Look! God's dwelling place is now among the people, and he will dwell with them. They will be his people, and God himself will be with them and be their God'" (v. 3).

Sam promised Annie a trip to Alaska. God promised us an eternity with Him.

Six months after Annie completed her last round of chemo, Sam and Annie stood on the deck of the Majestic Princess. Against a backdrop of snow capped mountains, they watched a pod of whales breech, sending sparkling water droplets high into the sky. Annie leaned back into Sam's strong embrace as he bent to whisper into her ear.

"See? I told you it would be wonderful."

"Yes, you did," Annie said. "You promised."

God promised too. The angel assured John, "These words are trustworthy and true" (22:6).

"And this is the testimony: God has given us eternal life, and this life is in his Son. Whoever has the Son has life; whoever does not have the Son of God does not have life. I write these things to you who believe in the name of the Son of God so that you may *know* that you have eternal life" (1 John 5:11–13, emphasis added).

Embrace the Truth: God, who cannot lie, promises we'll live in heaven with Him forever.

Declare Your Faith: Lord, I believe that when my life on this earth ends, I'll live with You for all eternity. What a glorious promise! Help me cling to this truth when I grow weary. Make this my anchor of hope: that no matter how hard my life becomes, I have an eternal future awaiting me—one with no sickness, no sorrow, no pain. One where I'll never cry again. Until that day, make me steadfast, immovable, always abounding in the work of the Lord. Help me live each day with eternity in mind. Even so, Lord, come quickly!

How to Have a Relationship with Christ

The Bible tells us how to enter into an eternal, transforming, life-giving relationship with Jesus. It begins by embracing a few foundational truths:

We must understand that we have sinned, and our sin grieves and separates us from our loving Father God.

> All have sinned and fall short of the glory of God. (Romans 3:23)

Because we are sinners, we are separated from God and deserve to die and spend eternity in hell.

> The wages of sin is death. (Romans 6:23)

We can't do anything to earn our place in heaven.

> It is by grace you have been saved, through faith—and this is not from yourselves, it is the gift of God—not by works, so that no one can boast. (Ephesians 2:8–9)

God loved us so much that He sacrificed His sinless, perfect Son, Jesus, to pay for our sin.

> God so loved the world that he gave his one and only Son, that whoever believes in him shall not perish but have eternal life. (John 3:16)

> God made him who had no sin to be sin for us, so that in him we might become the righteousness of God. (2 Corinthians 5:21)

We must be willing to repent of (turn away from) our sin and accept by faith what Jesus did for us on the cross. When we do this, God promises us a relationship with Him and a forever home in heaven.

> The gift of God is eternal life in Christ Jesus our Lord. (Romans 6:23)

If you want to have a relationship with God, tell Him. Here's a sample prayer:

> God, I know I'm a sinner who doesn't deserve a place in Your heaven. Today I repent of my sin. I surrender my life to You. I accept what Jesus did for me when He died on the cross. Come into my heart, God, and make me a new person.

If you prayed this prayer or said the same thing in your own words, and you really meant it, then God has something to say to you:

> If you declare with your mouth, "Jesus is Lord," and believe in your heart that God raised him from the dead, you will be saved. (Romans 10:9)

If you surrendered your life to Christ, I want to rejoice with you and help you on your way. Please drop me an email at LoriHatcher.com. For more encouragement, visit my blog, *Refresh*, at www.LoriHatcher.com.

Notes

1. To read more about Cape Fear Farmlife, visit https://capefearfarmlife.com/.
2. This line is from the hymn "Turn Your Eyes upon Jesus," which is in the public domain.
3. Matthew Henry, "Commentary on Psalms 42," Blue Letter Bible, https://www.blueletterbible.org/comm/mhc/psa/psa_042.cfm.
4. Ken Ham, "Earth: Just Right for Life," Answers in Genesis, April 3, 2016, https://answersingenesis.org/blogs/ken-ham/2016/04/03/earth-just-right-for-life.
5. "All Hail the Power of Jesus's Name," Edward Perronet, 1780.
6. Andrew Dragos, "6 Steps to Reading the Bible Like John Wesley," Seedbed, April 11, 2014, https://seedbed.com/6-steps-reading-bible-like-john-wesley.
7. "George Muller Persistent Prayer for 5 Individuals," *Devotional*, GeorgeMuller.org, July 3, 2017, https://www.georgemuller.org/devotional/george-muller-persistent-prayer-for-5-individuals.
8. Max Wade-Matthews and Wendy Thompson, *The Encyclopedia of Music: A Guide to the Greatest Composers and the Instruments of the Orchestra* (Dayton, OH: Lorenz Books, 2020), 85.
9. Read more of Jimmy's story at On the Rock Ministries, https://ontherockjimmy.org/.
10. Ludwig Bemelmans, *Madeline* (New York: Viking, 1967).
11. "G5293 - hypotassō - Strong's Greek Lexicon (NIV)," Blue Letter Bible, accessed April 1, 2025, https://www.blueletterbible.org/lexicon/g5293/niv/mgnt/0-1/.
12. Thomas Manton, *Crossway Classic Commentaries: James* (Wheaton, IL: Crossway Books, 1995), 251.

13. Manton, *James*, 253.
14. The quote seems to have originated with Elizabeth Stone in the mid 1980s, though worded a bit differently. However, I'm unable to locate exactly where and when the saying first appeared.
15. Tertullian, The Prescription against Heretics, Ch. 36, http://www.newadvent.org/fathers/0311.htm

About the Author

Lori Hatcher is an author, blogger, career health-care worker, freelance editor, and women's ministry speaker. She's the author of numerous devotional books, including *Refresh Your Hope: 60 Devotions for Trusting God with All Your Heart* and *Think on These Things: 60 Thoughtful Devotions for Renewed Peace.*

Lori's articles and devotions have appeared in numerous print and online publications including *Our Daily Bread*, *The Upper Room*, *Guideposts*, *Revive Our Hearts*, and *Crosswalk.com*. She's contributed to numerous compilations, including Guideposts' *All God's Creatures, Evenings with Jesus,* and *God Hears Her: A Joyful Christmas.*

A contest-winning Toastmasters International speaker (ACG, ALB), Lori uses high-impact stories to impart transformational truth. She often draws from her childhood in small-town Rhode Island, her work as a dental hygienist, and the spiritual insights she gains from her grandchildren to create touching stories that reveal God's love and character.

Lori believes the key to living a life of faith and joy depends on knowing, believing, and obeying God's Word. This is why she loves writing devotions that point readers to the truths of the Bible. She hopes *Lord, I Believe* will help you trust God, even when your faith wobbles.

If *Lord, I Believe* has blessed you, Lori would be most grateful if you'd leave a review on Amazon.com or your favorite book retailer. Thoughtful reviews help readers find great books.

If you'd like to learn more about Lori and her well-loved five-minute devotions, visit LoriHatcher.com.

renew, refresh, reclaim

In a world that disappoints again and again, your heavenly Father does not. Wherever you are today and whatever your situation tomorrow, know on a whole new level that God is with you, He is for you, and He will never fail you.

Well-loved author, blogger, and women's ministry speaker Lori Hatcher is here to help renew, refresh, and reclaim your confidence in the rock-solid truths about God.

Our Daily Bread Publishing®

refresh your hope
60 DEVOTIONS FOR TRUSTING GOD WITH ALL YOUR HEART
LORI HATCHER
refresh your faith
uncommon devotions from every book of the Bible
Lori Hatcher
refresh your prayers
uncommon devotions to restore power and praise
Lori Hatcher

Spread the Word by Doing One Thing.

- Give a copy of this book as a gift.
- Share the QR code link via your social media.
- Write a review of this book on your blog, favorite bookseller's website, or at ourdailybreadpublishing.org.
- Recommend this book to your church, small group, or book club.

Connect with us.

Our Daily Bread Publishing
PO Box 3566, Grand Rapids, MI 49501, USA
Email: books@odbm.org